ARIZONA'S

144

BY

JAMES

TALLON

BEST

CAMPGROUNDS

REVISED EDITION
FOURTH OVERALL PRINTING

A R I Z O N A ' S
CONTENTS
C A M P G R O U N D S

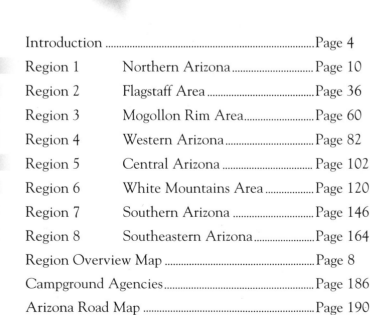

Campground Charts and Maps

Fishing Site Charts

Prepared by the Book Division of *Arizona Highways* magazine, a
monthly publication of the Arizona Department of Transportation.
www.arizonahighways.com
2039 West Lewis Avenue, Phoenix, Arizona 85009
(602) 712-2000; (800) 543-5432
Win Holden — Publisher
Bob Albano — Managing Editor
Evelyn Howell — Associate Editor
PK Perkin McMahon — Associate Editor
Peter Ensenberger — Director of Photography
Kim Ensenberger — Production Director

Book Editor — Wes Holden
Book Design — Gary Bennett
Additional Design/Production — Linda Longmire, Annette Phares
Still-life Photography — Carlton's Photographic

(FRONT COVER) *Buffalo Crossing campground;* see Page 130.
(BACK COVER, CLOCKWISE FROM TOP) *Jacob Lake in Kaibab National Forest,
Bonita at Sunset Crater, Buffalo Crossing on East Fork of Black River,
and Hospital Flat on Mount Graham.*

(CONTENTS PAGES, CLOCKWISE FROM TOP LEFT) *Maple leaf, pronghorn antelope,
hawk feather, blue heron, ponderosa pinecone, black-tail jackrabbit.*

ARIZONA'S
INTRODUCTION
CAMPGROUNDS

W hat makes a campground a *best campground?* Ask a dozen campers and you'll get a dozen different answers. Some gregarious city dwellers may be intimidated by a companionless camping experience. Unfamiliar with the "wilderness," they may find the sound of a coyote's howl enough to send them packing for home. Seeking safety in numbers, these campers often can tolerate, perhaps even enjoy, company nearby. Other campers find it extremely irritating if campsites are close together, and rate the quality of their camping experience by how much wildlife they see and hear.

Some campers cannot leave certain comforts behind and won't camp where there aren't hot showers. Others

(OPPOSITE AND ABOVE) *Sunset brings camping's magic hour along the lower Colorado River where shoreline camping attracts boaters and anglers.*

find the best spots have only fire rings for amenities.

Some campers require a lake or stream just outside their tent, while others claim their best camp is amid a stand of saguaros with no flowing water for miles.

There are campers who hate paved loop drives through the campgrounds. (These are increasingly common in high-use campgrounds.) "It's not like you're really away from civilization with blacktop next to your campsite," one says. But others prefer pavement: "It prevents a steak you are grilling from being dusted when traffic goes by."

The more people I talked to, the more aware I became of personal preferences and variables. Knowing the impossibility of selecting campgrounds that would please everybody, I did what any normal writer-camper would do: I gave up.

The campgrounds in this book were selected with the author's unabashed bias. The initial factor determining which sites to include was how a given campground "felt" to me. As a romantic escapist eager to get away from congestion, noise, and some of the other negatives of the big city, I was guided chiefly by ambiance, pulchritude, and serenity. In my opinion, certain mountains aren't any less magnificent because there is

a pit toilet within a stone's throw of my camp. At another campground, I was put off by the trash scattered around. I sat at the picnic table quietly evaluating the situation, when a pair of tassel-eared Abert squirrels undulated into view, playing some sort of game among the ponderosas. I decided I could pick up a little litter to improve things. And it turned an okay camp into a great one.

Several campgrounds that had crystal streams running through them get more "pressure" than I like. Still, regularly I saw dark shadows of trout darting over the gravel. (Gad, my fly rod has been neglected too long.) I included all of the sites! (Streams tumbling through campgrounds may soon be only memories. More and more, the Forest Service and other agencies are moving campgrounds back from shorelines, citing increased human pollution as the reason, and justifiably so.)

Camping is not necessarily synonymous with being in the forest among conifers. The Arizona desert offers wondrous places to throw down a bedroll or park an RV. The raucous squawk of cactus wrens, the smell of creosote bushes after a rain shower, unique cacti like the saguaro, and sunsets of staggering beauty cannot be ignored — and once experienced, never forgotten. In selecting campgrounds, I tried to consider a broad spectrum, from campers who need only a ground cloth and a sleeping bag, through the rank and file, to those at the top of the comfort chain in motor homes with two bedrooms and 1½ baths. If you're longer than 45 feet, call the campgrounds to be sure you'll fit.

Our 144 sites are grouped into eight regions (see map on Page 8). Other maps locate each camping site, and charts summarize amenities and provide information for contacting management agencies regarding fees, permits, and campground status. Other charts summarize fishing and boating opportunities.

CHECK FIRST

Arizona Highways urges campers to check with management agencies for possible changes in campground status. Sometimes campgrounds are closed temporarily because of wildfires, renovations, or other factors. The "seasons of use" listed in charts for each region can vary with the weather, and campers are urged to call or check Internet Web sites to determine exact opening and closing dates. The charts contain codes identifying management agencies, listed on pages 186-192.

James Tallon has roamed, written about, and photographed Arizona's backcountry for more than 35 years. In conducting research for this book, he spent a year and a half visiting more than 215 campgrounds. For this edition, information about each campground was reviewed and revised as necessary.

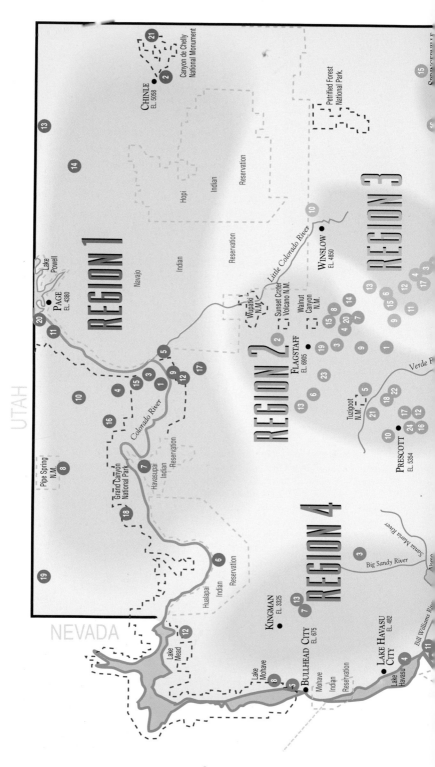

8

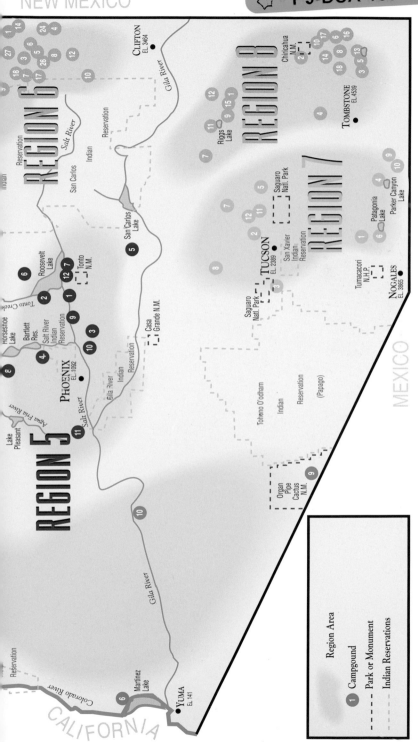

NORTHERN ARIZONA
REGION 1
CAMPGROUNDS

C amping Region 1 zigzags through the top one-fifth of Arizona, touching the borders of Nevada, Utah, and New Mexico. Inside its boundaries lie 22,000 square miles of scenery unmatched anywhere else on planet Earth. For starters, there are the world-favorite destinations: the Grand Canyon, Lake Powell, Monument Valley, Canyon de Chelly, and the Painted Desert, plus Vermilion Cliffs, Marble and Glen canyons, the North Kaibab National Forest, and that "you can't get there from here" place called the Arizona Strip. And don't forget the Kaibab, Navajo, Havasupai, and Hualapai Indian reservations.

Some campgrounds sit smack in the middle of the sunshine and scenery, like Lee's Ferry on the Colorado River in the depths of the Grand Canyon, where, so they say, the only part of you that doesn't get sun tanned is the roof of your mouth. Other places, like DeMotte, hide you in forest so dense you need a compass to find the restrooms. From the rims of the Grand Canyon, you can read all five chapters of Earth's geologic history. The 14-mile stretch of Colorado River between Glen Canyon Dam and Lee's Ferry has gained international recognition for its exceptional trout fishing. Antelope play on

(OPPOSITE) *Rim sitters at Point Imperial on the North Rim of the Grand Canyon gaze at Hayden Butte. At more than 8,000 feet elevation, the North Rim provides a cool, remote retreat for summer campers. Campgrounds in the area fill quickly, so it's best to make reservations well in advance.*

(ABOVE) *Hundreds of narrow, winding, water-filled inlets and slot canyons penetrate the slick rock shoreline of Lake Powell. A boater can spend a lifetime exploring wonders of the lake.*

the Arizona Strip, and buffalo roam on a ranch there. Up on the Kaibab Plateau, it's Canadian-like amid spruce, fir, pine, and aspen forests with sun-dappled meadows.

The list goes on and on. There's a lot of driving to be done in Region 1, and you'll yearn for much more than your standard summer vacation to even begin to explore its uniqueness.

❶ The trek to **BRIGHT ANGEL** campground at the bottom of the Grand Canyon is not easy, even for the resolute hiker. From the South Rim's Grand Canyon Village via Bright Angel Trail, it's a 9.3-mile hike. From the North Rim, it's 14 downhill miles. But it isn't the distance *in* that makes it tough, it's the distance *out*. At the bottom of the Canyon, and less than a mile up Bright Angel Creek from the campground, is Phantom Ranch. People come from around the world to ride a mule to this remote place. I always enjoy the hike. Despite the physical demands necessary to get here, you'll never forget the beauty, tranquillity, and uniqueness of Bright Angel campground. The creek tumbles alongside, a gentle breeze rustles through 100-foot-tall cottonwood trees, the great walls of the Canyon seem to reach upward forever, and the campground is surrounded by Vishnu  schist, among the Earth's oldest rocks. High-jumping rainbow trout and secretive browns swim in Bright Angel's cold, clear water. The size of some of the fish in this small creek surprises most people, who don't realize that much of the fish's growing is done in the Colorado River just a few hundred yards away. It is essential to apply for a backcountry camping permit months in advance to reserve your date choice (see Page 192).

❷ **COTTONWOOD** campground, just inside the boundary of Canyon de Chelly National Monument, is — as you would expect — shaded by cottonwood trees. Tall and graceful, the cottonwood canopy imparts an ambiance campers love — particularly in autumn, when the leaves turn golden, sunny days linger with comfortable warmth, and brisk evenings make campfires even more inviting. The campground butts up against Chinle, a bustling community of about 5,500 people where food, lodging, and other services are available. At Canyon de Chelly, the National Park Service administers the campground and the monument, but the land belongs to the Navajo Tribe. Numerous Navajo families live in the canyon.

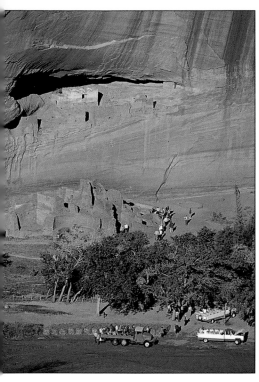

From overlooks — some accessible to handicapped visitors — you'll see their homes, corn fields, and flocks of sheep far below on the canyon floor. To preserve the residents' privacy, you must have a local guide to enter the canyon to see sights such as Kokopelli Cave, Petroglyph Rock, First Ruin, Junction Ruin, Ceremonial Cave, and Ledge Ruin. The only exception is the hiking trail to White House Ruin, which you can hike alone. For information about the campground, the monument, and four-wheel-drive, horseback, or hiking tours. go to the visitors center, about 3 miles east of U.S. 191 along Navajo Route 7. The center also displays exhibits telling the story of people who moved into Canyon de Chelly more than 1,800 years ago and stayed for 1,100 years before abandoning the area.

③ COTTONWOOD CAMP sits on the east bank of Bright Angel Creek, 6.8 miles down the Kaibab Trail from the Grand Canyon's North Rim. (The hike in, with a pack on your back,

Text continued on page 20

(OPPOSITE) *The unique view of the Bright Angel Trail from between a mule's flopping ears leaves an unforgetable Grand Canyon memory.*
(ABOVE) *Accessible by trail from the south rim of Canyon de Chelly, White House Ruin is the only dwelling visitors can explore without a guide.*

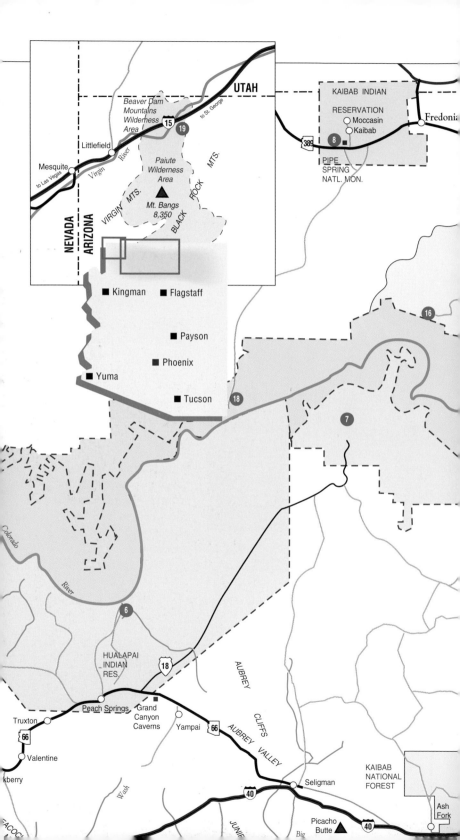

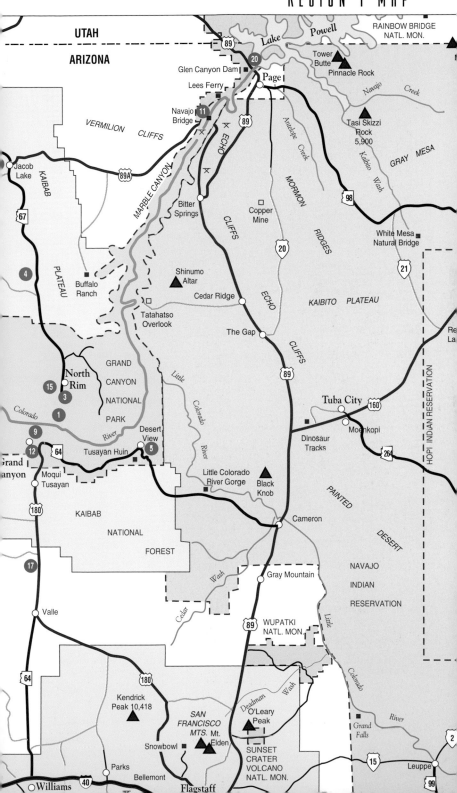

REGION 1 — RECREATION SITES

D Dispersed Camping
* Handicapped access
^ Tents only

#	Site	APPROX. ELEVATION	SEASONS OF USE ■	DAYS - LIMIT	FEE	APPROX. NO. OF UNITS	TRAILER LIMIT (FT.)	FACILITIES				CONTACT INFORMATION ■
								SAFE WATER	RV DUMP STATION	RESTROOMS	SHOWERS	
1	^Bright Angel	2400	All Yr.	2	●	33		●	●	●		NPS4A
2	*Cottonwood	5500	All Yr.	5		96	35	●	●	●		NPS1
3	^Cottonwood Camp	4000	All Yr.	2	●	25				●		NPS4A
4	Demotte	8800	May Oct.	14	▲	22	22	●		●		NFS4A
5	Desert View	6700	May Oct.	7	●	50	30	●		●		NPS4B
6	Diamond Creek	1900	All Yr.	Call	●	D				●		IR5
7	^Havasupai	3500	All Yr.	Call	●	250				●		IR2
8	Kaibab-Paiute Campground & RV Park	4900	Apr Oct.	Call	●	47	30	●		●	●	IR3
9	^Indian Garden	3800	All Yr.	2	●	35		●		●		NPS4A
10	*Jacob Lake	7900	May Oct.	14	●	53	32	●	●	●		NFS4A
11	*Lee's Ferry	3400	All Yr.	14	●	51		●	●	●		NPS3
12	*Mather	6900	All Yr.	7	●	317	30	●	●	●	●	NPS4B
13	*Mitten View	5600	All Yr.		●	100		●	●	●	●	IR4A
14	Navajo Nat'l Mon.	7300	All Yr.	7		47	28	●		●		NPS6
15	*North Rim	8200	May Oct.	14	●	82	30	●	●	●	●	NPS4B
16	^Indian Hollow	6300	May Nov.	14		3				●		NFS4A
17	*Ten -X	6600	May Oct.	14	●	70	40	●		●		NFS4B
18	Toroweap Point	4600	May Oct.	14	●	11				●		NPS4B
19	*Virgin River	2400	All Yr.	90	●	75	45	●		●		BLM1
20	*Wahweap	3800	All Yr.	14	●	180	45	●	●	●	●	NPS3
21	Wheatfields Lake	7000	May Oct.	14	●	25	Call			●		IR4B

▲ Closed for renovation until 2006 season. Call (928) 643-7395 for reopening information.

■ Dates are approximate. Check with managing agencies if you are planning a trip near the start or end of the season. Contact information is on pages 186-192, where management agencies are listed alphabetically. The first two or three letters in the code for each campground designate the agency. The number and letters following the initial letters designate regions or districts.

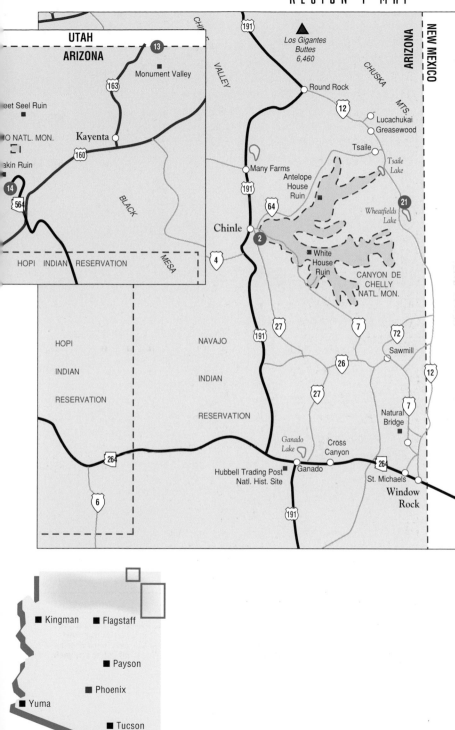

UTAH

ARIZONA

Monument Valley

163

eet Seel Ruin

O NATL. MON.

Kayenta

160

akin Ruin

14

564

HOPI INDIAN RESERVATION

BLACK

MESA

13

CHI VALLEY

191

Los Gigantes
Buttes
6,460

Round Rock

12

CHUSKA

MTS.

Lucachukai

Greasewood

Tsaile

Tsaile
Lake

Many Farms

191

Antelope
House
Ruin

64

Chinle

2

Wheatfields
Lake

21

4

White
House
Ruin

CANYON DE
CHELLY
NATL. MON.

ARIZONA

NEW MEXICO

HOPI

INDIAN

RESERVATION

NAVAJO

INDIAN

RESERVATION

191

27

26

27

7

7

72

Sawmill

12

Natural
Bridge

264

6

Ganado
Lake

Cross
Canyon

Hubbell Trading Post
Natl. Hist. Site

Ganado

264

St. Michaels

Window
Rock

191

■ Kingman   ■ Flagstaff

■ Payson

■ Phoenix

■ Yuma

■ Tucson

Text continued from Page 15

will give new meaning to the term "rubber legs.") Maj. John Wesley Powell walked the banks of this stream during his epic 1869 exploration of the Grand Canyon. Bright Angel was so named because of its sharp contrast with the "Dirty Devil" stream that Powell encountered previously. En route you will

pass Roaring Springs, the source of Bright Angel Creek. And just 1.5 miles downstream from Cottonwood is Ribbon Falls. Seven miles down-trail from Cottonwood is Bright Angel campground and the Colorado River. Get your backcountry camping permits months in advance. If you like to fish unusual places, this one sure fits the description. Both rainbow and brown trout swim in Bright Angel Creek.

❹ DeMotte, just off State Route 67 about 25 miles south of Jacob Lake and 7 miles north of the entrance to Grand Canyon National Park's North Rim, hides on a hillside in a Canadian-type forest of Douglas fir, Engelmann and blue spruce, and quaking aspen. This may be the epitome of camping envisioned by most outdoor people. At 8,800 feet,

DeMotte ranks as one of Arizona's highest campgrounds. Surrounding forest scenery makes getting here, via one of the prettiest drives in the United States, a memorable experience. Mornings and evenings, in the pastoral setting of DeMotte Park, deer regularly browse and wild turkeys peck at grasshoppers. Considered an "overflow" campground for the Grand Canyon's North Rim, the wilderness feel of DeMotte is preferred by many visitors who are undisturbed by the more limited access to other Canyon facilities. In case you don't feel like doing any camp cooking, there is a resort with a restaurant just a short walk from the campground. And nearby concessionaires provide guided hiking and horseback riding.

⑤ **DESERT VIEW** campground, 26 miles east of Grand Canyon Village along State Route 64, yields fantastic views of the Canyon at its widest point, about 15 miles, and also of western portions of the Painted Desert and Navajo Indian Reservation. The campground's paved roads loop easily amid fragrant junipers and delicate Apache plumes. To the west rises Desert View Watchtower, a composite replica of Ancestral Puebloan towers found throughout the Four Corners region. It was near Moran Point, in 1540, that Garcia Lopez de Cardenas, Pedro de Tovar, and a group of Spanish conquistadors reined their horses to a halt and became the first non-Indians to see the "world's most sublime spectacle."

⑥ **DIAMOND CREEK** campground, on the Hualapai Indian Reservation about 21 miles north of Peach Springs, is at the bottom of the Grand Canyon. Virtually unknown is the fact that this is the only place a person can drive to the Canyon's floor. En route you travel through geologic pages of the Earth's history, from Paleozoic to Precambrian eras. Although you are not actually in Grand Canyon National Park, the camp lies

(OPPOSITE, TOP) *Phantom Ranch near Bright Angel campground offers a dormitory and cabins for those who require more comfort than a tent provides.*
(OPPOSITE) *A stay at DeMotte campground often includes a view of the flocks of wild turkey that roam the forests and meadows of the Kaibab Plateau.*
(ABOVE) *Diamond Creek campground at the bottom of Grand Canyon.*

just across the Colorado River from the sandy mouth of Diamond Creek. The road from Peach Springs, as you might suspect, is downhill all the way, dropping from 4,791 feet to less than 2,000 feet where Diamond Creek enters the river. The unpaved road, passes along the rocky bed of Diamond Creek. From there on, driving it requires a high-clearance vehicle. Four-wheel drive is better. Caution: You must make several stream crossings and actually drive in water down cattail-lined portions of Diamond Creek. This can be a dangerous flash-flood situation during inclement weather. Being walled in by the steep-sided Inner Gorge limits access to fishing, but some of Arizona's biggest rainbow trout pass Diamond Creek on their way upstream. Other game fish, such as largemouth bass and channel catfish, also occasionally negotiate their way upstream from Lake Mead.

7 HAVASUPAI campground lies in Havasu Canyon at the end of an 8-mile-long trail, which begins at the end of a 60-mile drive on Indian Route 18. The home of the Havasupai

Indians, the canyon is an almost magical place, where the turquoise waters of Havasu Creek plunge over four great waterfalls en route to the Colorado River. The actual campground extends for about three-fourths of a mile creekside between Havasu Falls and Mooney Falls. Although in the Grand Canyon, the Havasupai Indian Reservation is not part of the national park. You can hike or ride horseback into this spectacular campground, but reservations are required. Make your plans months in advance because demand is heavy. Contact: Havasupai Tourist Enterprises, General Delivery, Supai, AZ 86435, or call (928) 448-2121 or (928) 448-2141. For lodging, call (928) 448-2111.

(OPPOSITE) *The travertine-laden waters of Havasu Creek plunge 150 feet to form the pools below Havasu Falls in the western Grand Canyon.*
(ABOVE) *An aerial view of the trail to Havasu shows how it drops steeply the first mile and a half, then descends gradually along the canyon floor for seven more miles.*

8 You'll find **KAIBAB-PAIUTE TRIBE** RV park and campground about a mile off State Route 389 along Moccasin Road just across from Pipe Spring National Monument, a former Mormon fort. Located on the Kaibab-Paiute Indian Reserva-

tion, 15 miles west of Fredonia, and somewhat overgrown with sagebrush, this is a true Western base camp for seeing this part of Arizona. A sign says to pick a site and (eventually) someone will come by to collect a fee. En route to or from the community of Fredonia, you pass Shiprock, a massive, red- and buff-colored formation that reaches 5,048 feet above sea level. This vast region is called the Arizona Strip, which, except for two bridges, is cut off from the rest of the state by Glen, Marble, and Grand canyons. It is wide-open country, and never more so than at night when the sky seems overflowing with stars.

9 **INDIAN GARDEN** campground is not served by a road. It sits about 3,000 feet straight down from the limestone ramparts of the Grand Canyon's South Rim. The hike to it is 4.6 miles via the switchbacks of Bright Angel Trail. Want to see where you're going to camp? Indian Garden is visible from several viewpoints along the West Rim Drive on the South Rim. Those "little bushes" down there are cottonwood trees. The camp is used mostly by hikers going to or from Phantom Ranch at the bottom of the Canyon or on a leisurely schedule to other points in the Canyon, perhaps the North Rim. The Park Service limits the number of campers so be sure to make reservations early. Bright Angel Trail is used by mules as well as by hikers. The trip is not easy for hikers or mules. But remember, it doesn't matter whether the mules are going up or down the trail, they always get the inside. For the rugged individual, the few negatives associated with camping at Indian Garden is far offset by the phenomenal views.

10 JACOB LAKE campground, at the junction of State Route 67 and U.S. Route 89A, is located at what has been one of Arizona's landmark crossroads for more than a hundred years. The camp is in an open grove of ponderosa pines right across the road from Jacob Lake Lodge, which includes a restaurant, gas station, and store. The "lake," really a shallow pond about a mile away, was named for Jacob Hamblin, a Mormon missionary who explored these highlands during the 1860s and 70s. If you head south on State Route 67 — now designated by the State of Arizona as a scenic route — for about 45 miles, you'll be at the North Rim of the Grand Canyon. A word to the wise: During the busy summer season, Jacob Lake campground is inundated by visitors bound for the North Rim. On finding facilities at the latter full, they backtrack to DeMotte and Jacob Lake camps, which themselves often fill up by midmorning.

11 LEE'S FERRY campground is 5 sensationally scenic miles into Glen Canyon National Recreation Area off U.S. Route 89A. Watch for signs and turn north (right) after crossing Navajo Bridge over Marble Canyon. The nearby settlement of

Marble Canyon includes a gas station, a fishing shop, and basic supplies. The campground occupies a gentle slope on the west bank of the Colorado River below the magnificent Vermilion Cliffs. From the boat ramp, you can see a trail that zigzags up the opposite wall of Glen Canyon. Just a mile away is the embarkation point for float trips through the Grand Canyon. In 1872, Mormon pioneer John D. Lee established a ferry here for crossing the then-untamed Colorado River, the only crossing for hundreds of miles. One of Lee's several wives, Emma, ran the ferry during his many absences. During those early days, the ferry crossing became famous

---

(OPPOSITE) *Preserved today at Pipe Spring National Monument, "Winsor Castle," built by Mormon pioneers, surrounds the area's only reliable water.*
(ABOVE) *Catching lunker trout is an everyday occurrence at Lee's Ferry on the Colorado River below Glen Canyon Dam.*

as part of the Honeymoon Trail used by young Mormon couples traveling by wagon from Arizona to St. George, Utah, to have their marriages sanctified in the temple. The 14 miles of Colorado River upstream to Glen Canyon Dam have acquired considerable fame for consistently producing rainbow trout up to 16 pounds. Only artificial lures and flies with barbless hooks

may be used. Check the Arizona Game and Fish (www.gf.state.az.us) regulations for current possession limits.

⑫ From **MATHER** campground, near Grand Canyon Village on the South Rim, you can walk to the visitors center, restaurants, general store, showers, laundromat, and gift shops, as well as to many of the often-overlooked Rim trails. Even though Mather has more than 300 sites, the crush of 4.5 million people visiting Grand Canyon annually (most in summer) makes campground reservations essential. At the 7,000-foot elevation, you find a mix of ponderosa and piñon pines, and Gambel oaks. The Abert squirrel and its look-alike relative, the North Rim's Kaibab squirrel, are prime examples of evolution. Eons ago, before the Grand Canyon separated them, they were members of the same species. A careful observer will note the different color characteristics the two have developed. Officials named the campground and Mather Point, one of Grand Canyon's most spectacular, for Stephen Mather, a pioneering member of the National Park Service.

⓭ **MITTEN VIEW** campground offers one of the best panoramas of any campground on the planet. Situated on a prominence overlooking Monument Valley near the entrance to the Navajo tribal park, this is the perfect place to watch sunsets and sunrises and feel the presence of this dramatic landscape. Towering spires, mesas, and buttes prompted the name

Monument Valley. It's hard to believe the area once was a lowland basin. Over millions of years, natural forces created the monuments, layer by layer, and added colors that change as the sun and clouds move across the sky. You might have trouble sleeping, however, as you'll probably want to stay up all night and watch the stars. This remarkable part of the Navajo Indian Reservation was virtually unknown until it was made famous by the John Ford/John Wayne movies *Fort Apache*, *She Wore a Yellow Ribbon*, and *The Searchers*. You can take a self-guided tour through part of the valley with a conventional two-wheel-drive vehicle. Inquire at the visitors center for information about guided, four-wheel-drive tours into the valley's outback for still more awe-inspiring views. From U.S. Route 160 at Kayenta, drive 50 miles north on U.S. Route 163.

(OPPOSITE) *Eons of erosion carved the precarious perches for the balanced rocks at the base of the Vermilion Cliffs above Lees Ferry.*
(ABOVE) *Tent campers pitch their portable homes before some of the West's most recognizable scenery in Monument Valley.*

⑭ NAVAJO NATIONAL MONUMENT visitors center and two campgrounds are surrounded by piñon pines and junipers at the lip of a mesa overlooking Tsegi Canyon. This is a great place to camp and explore prehistoric ruins. In order to hike 5 miles round-trip with a ranger into Betatakin Ruins, check with the visitors center immediately upon arrival. The 134-room Ancestral Puebloan cliff dwelling of Betatakin (Hillside House) lies in an immense alcove that has a ceiling 450 feet high and a width of 375 feet. Keet Seel (Broken Pottery), one of the best ruins in the Southwest, lies 8.5 miles from the visi-

tors center. To hike to Keet Seel make reservations (928-672-2700) up to five months ahead. A ranger will meet visitors at the Keet Seel site. From U.S. Route 160 between Tuba City and Kayenta, take State Route 564 north about 9 miles to reach the monument and campgrounds.

⑮ **NORTH RIM** campground, at Grand Canyon National Park (turn right off State Route 67 just before you get to the lodge), provides the opportunity to sip sunrise coffee amid a grove of red-barked ponderosas right on the Canyon's rim. Reservations required. From your campsite you can savor the most spectacular manifestation of erosion in the world. Rim trails take off from here, and park specialists give evening talks on geology, flora, fauna, and related subjects in the nearby amphitheater. Sure to be mentioned are the tassel-eared Kaibab squirrels that scurry about the campground. Not surprisingly, their lifestyle is inextricably connected to the ponderosa pine. Don't be startled if deer walk into camp, but override the temptation to give them a handout. This is a no-no! Not only is it unhealthy for wild deer, but it causes them to become dependent on people. Convenient to the campground are restaurants, gift shops, a general store, laundry, and showers.

16 Kaibab Plateau's **INDIAN HOLLOW** begins a North Rim retreat for serious outdoor folks. Morning or late afternoon travel through 35 miles of conifers and aspens nearly guarantees seeing turkeys or deer. From State 67 at Jacob Lake, turn west on Forest Service Road 579 to FR 461, take FR 461/462 to FR 422, FR 422 south to FR 425, southwest on FR 425, then west on FR 232 to the campsites at road's end. Mostly all-weather roads, about 4 miles of FR 232 need high clearance. A good base camp for Thunder River hikes in the Canyon or short back-road treks. Overflow camping in the open forest.

17 **TEN-X** campground, just off U.S. Route 180 about 4 miles south of the Grand Canyon National Park boundary, was once cowboy country. The Ten-X brand belonged to an area ranch. Where campers now bed down, cattle and cowboys on horseback once trod. Beautifully set amid ponderosas, piñons, and junipers, this campground mainly serves the seasonal overflow of Grand Canyon visitors. A couple of miles north of Ten-X, you'll find the thriving community of Tusayan. Once a corral, horse pasture, and outback saloon, Tusayan now includes Grand Canyon Airport, helicopter ports, an IMAX theater, motels, restaurants, stores, service stations, and curio shops. Perhaps of more interest to the outdoor person, Forest Service Road 302 going east out of Tusayan makes a semicircle of about 14 miles to intercept State Route 64 at Grandview Point. Several other back roads connect to FR 302, and exploratory trips provide excellent opportunities to see deer, tassel-eared squirrels, coyotes, and other wildlife.

(OPPOSITE) *Keet Seel, one of three spectacular Ancestral Puebloan ruins protected at Navajo National Monument, was abandoned nearly 700 years ago.* (ABOVE) *A Kaibab squirrel, found only on the Kaibab Plateau north of the Grand Canyon, resembles the Abert squirrel in every way but coloration.*

18 TOROWEAP POINT campground (also called "Tuweep"), about 60 miles south of State Route 389 on a primitive Arizona Strip road, has only 11 units, but the "Campground Full" sign is seldom if ever hung out. Only rugged individualists want to stray that far from the pavement. Take a good map and heed a word of caution: Rain can turn dust to "grease" on the road surface, making travel impossible even for four-wheel-drive vehicles. (Believe it!) The campground, which lies in a rocky scrubland setting (so bring your own firewood), is about a mile from one of the most staggering, heart-palpitating, scenic views in the world. Here the Grand Canyon drops 3,000 feet straight down to the Colorado River and Lava Falls, among the most dangerous rapids in the Canyon. The turnoff from State 389 is about 9 miles west of Fredonia.

19 VIRGIN RIVER campground is reached from Interstate 15 (Exit 18, also called Cedar Pockets Interchange) where it cuts across the northwest corner of Arizona. Access I-15 from St. George, Utah, or Mesquite, Nev. It's the only developed campground on the Arizona Strip. The Virgin River Canyon recreation area perches on a low hill inside a basin of the Virgin Mountains. The area includes day-use facilities and access to hiking trails. Joshua trees decorate the slopes adding to a somewhat surreal landscape, and the Virgin River flows by before emptying into Lake Mead. Noting the small size of the river, you can't help but wonder how it ever sliced through the formidable Virgin Mountains. The sun rises a little late here because of the surrounding peaks, so you'll easily be up to watch it work on the colors in the canyon. On our last visit, the campground host told us he'd lived here six years and liked it so much that "the only way they'll ever get me to leave is with dynamite."

(OPPOSITE) *Toroweap Point, at the end of nearly 80 miles of dirt road, offers a 3,000-foot straight-down view of Lava Falls in the Grand Canyon.* (ABOVE) *An erosion-carved land of colorful rock and blue skies can be found in the Virgin River Gorge in the high desert of northwestern Arizona.*

㉑ **WAHWEAP** campground, on the Lake Powell shoreline just off U.S. Route 89, provides exceptional views of this incredible "man-influenced" spectacle. Impounded by Glen Canyon Dam, the lake attracts water-oriented recreationists in swarms, and for good reason. Everywhere you look, the carved-rock scenery is awe-inspiring. A rental houseboat or tour-boat trip up-lake to Rainbow Bridge, the highest natural bridge span on Earth, always draws accolades from impressed visitors. The lake is named for Maj. John Wesley Powell, the one-armed Civil War veteran who explored Glen, Marble, and Grand canyons back in 1869. The second-largest reservoir in North America, Lake Powell has nearly 2,000 miles of shoreline. It's fish population includes bass — striped, largemouth, and smallmouth — walleye, northern pike, catfish, and crappie and

other panfish. Each season of the year presents fish-catching opportunities and challenges for one species or another. Striped bass in the 30-pound class are not uncommon. The record largemouth exceeded 10 pounds, and the record small-mouth topped 5 pounds. Everything you'd ever want while in the camping mode probably can be found at Lake Powell Resort and Marina. But on the rare chance you can't find it there, the community of Page, just a couple of miles away, is sure to have supplies you need. For houseboat-renting and tour information call (800) 528-6154, or visit www.lakepowell.com.

(ABOVE) *At Lake Powell Marina, passengers board tour boats bound for Rainbow Bridge National Monument and other attractions on the 180-mile-long lake.*

REGION 1 FISHING

	Bright Angel Creek	Lake Mead	Pearce Ferry	South Cove	Temple Bar	Lake Mohave	Colorado River (below Mohave, Arizona Side)	Katherine Landing	Willow Beach
FACILITIES									
BOAT RENTAL		●			●	●		●	●
MOTOR LIMITS									
BOATS ALLOWED		●	●	●	●	●	●	●	●
CAMP NEARBY		●	●			●	●	●	●
STORE		●			●	●	●	●	●
FISH SPECIES									
BULLHEAD									
WALLEYE									
NORTHERN PIKE									
CATFISH (Flathead)									
CATFISH (Channel)		●	●	●	●	●	●	●	●
SUNFISH		●	●	●	●	●	●	●	●
CRAPPIE		●	●	●	●	●	●	●	
STRIPED BASS		●	●	●	●	●	●	●	●
WHITE BASS									
SM.MOUTH BASS		●							
LG.MOUTH BASS		●	●	●	●	●	●	●	●
CUTTHROAT									
GRAYLING									
BROOK	●								
NATIVE									
BROWN	●								
RAINBOW	●					●	●	●	●
FLY & LURE ONLY									
ELEVATION	2600	1200				645	645		
AVERAGE DEPTH (IN FEET)		280				75			
AVERAGE ACREAGE		110,000				26,500			

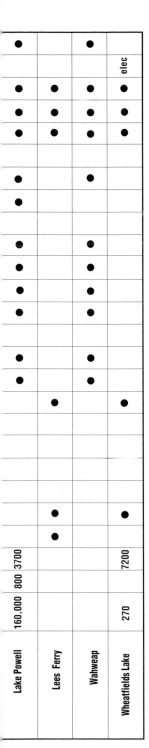

	Lake Powell	Lees Ferry	Wahweap	Wheatfields Lake
	•		•	
elec	•	•	•	•
	•	•	•	•
	•	•	•	•
	•		•	
	•			
	•		•	
	•		•	
	•		•	
	•		•	
	•		•	
	•		•	
			•	•
			•	•
			•	
	160,000	800	3700	7200
			270	

21 **WHEATFIELDS LAKE** campground is on one side of Indian Route 12, and the lake is on the other. Self-contained RVers will find the campground, located in an open forest of ponderosa pines at an elevation of 7,200 feet, primitive. Space always seems to be available. Camping amid these cool pines offers an oasis-like departure from the treeless flats of the surrounding Painted Desert. Nearby Black Pinnacle, a 7,850-foot

rocky prominence, resembles Devil's Tower in Wyoming. Despite great scenery and nearby attractions like Canyon de Chelly National Monument, just west on Indian Route 64, most Wheatfields campers have fishing in mind. In the relatively waterless Navajo Nation, Wheatfields Lake has developed into an excellent trout fishery. When using a lure or fly, it is not uncommon to hook a fish, lose it, then get another strike before you can finish the retrieve. The Navajos operate a lakeside store that offers camping and fishing necessities.

(ABOVE) *Wheatfields Lake offers the camper a casual, scenic campground, and the angler rainbow, brook, and cutthroat trout. Wheatfields is among the most popular lakes on the Navajo Indian Reservation.*

REGION 2
CAMPGROUNDS

Camping in Region 2 has its ups and downs, so to speak. The elevation near Bonito campground at Sunset Crater Volcano National Monument is about 7,000 feet. Oak Creek Canyon camps range around 5,000 feet, and Dead Horse Ranch about 3,300 feet. Up on Mingus Mountain, Potato Patch campground nears 7,000 feet, while down at Beaver Creek it's 4,500 feet. Crown King in the Bradshaw Mountains has some campgrounds at 6,000 feet — well, you get the picture.

This region takes in portions of three national forests, Coconino, Kaibab, and Prescott, which should be enough to satisfy those who feel they aren't camping unless they're surrounded by trees. It may also enlighten some out-of-state campers to the fact that Arizona is much more than just cactus country and sand dunes.

Oak Creek Canyon, with its dramatic red- and buff-colored walls, provides some of the most popular camping in the region. An impressive number of Europeans rent RVs at their ports of entry and include the campgrounds in Oak Creek Canyon among their top destinations.

In addition to the forests and the scenery of red rock country, this region also boasts five national monuments and the old

(OPPOSITE) *A tent-trailer combines comfort and convenience at Pine Flat campground in the upper reaches of Oak Creek Canyon. Pine Flat provides a base for a number of hikes in the Oak Creek area, including the spectacular and extremely popular West Fork trail.*

(ABOVE) *One of the more-easily recognized monuments in red rock country, Bell Rock rises adjacent to U.S. Route 89A near Sedona. Bell Rock is regarded as a vortex, or place of energy and power, by New Age followers who visit a number of these sites in the area.*

hillside ghost town of Jerome. One final thought: Don't go anywhere without your hiking shoes and/or your fishing rod.

① **BEAVER CREEK** campground, northeast of McGuireville, is 3 miles southeast of Interstate 17 (exit 298) on Forest Service Road 618. The campground overlooks Wet Beaver Creek, a perennial stream. Although mesquite, prickly pear cacti, and yucca grow in the surrounding countryside, Beaver Creek campground sits in a shady pocket of sycamores and cot-

tonwoods. Prehistoric Sinagua Indians lived in the region between the 12th and 15th centuries. Nearby Montezuma Castle National Monument and Montezuma Well display and interpret evidence of their considerable skills at hunting, gathering, and farming. Spring and fall camping is most comfortable at this 3,800-foot elevation. Hikers and backpackers find trails into Wet Beaver Wilderness close by. Using this camp as their base, fisher folk work the creek for rainbow trout.

② **BONITO** campground lies next to Sunset Crater Volcano National Monument amid the San Francisco Volcanic Field. Drive 12 miles northeast of Flagstaff on U.S. Route 89, turn east on Forest Service Road 545, and drive 2 miles to the site. Paved loops weave among ponderosa pines and Apache plumes in an austere cinderland beauty. Tassel-eared Abert squirrels and the ever-active Steller's jay make their homes here. In the monument's "lunar-scape" volcanic vastness NASA trained the U.S. astronauts who flew to the moon. Above the campsites, the 1,000-foot-high cone of Sunset Crater peeps through the pines. It erupted in the winter of 1064-65, and temporarily ran off the local prehistoric residents, the Sinagua. When the volcano went back to sleep, these farmers returned in greater numbers than ever and built what today we call Wupatki National Monument.

❸ You'll find CAVE SPRINGS campground 12 miles north of Sedona on State Route 89A near the mouth of the comely canyon of the West Fork of Oak Creek. An exceptionally varied trail, specially flavored with geological and botanical points of interest, winds comfortably up thickly forested West Fork Canyon. Historically, author Zane Grey was enamored with this area (as so many of us are) and spent a considerable length of time here writing *The Call of The Canyon*. The ruins at the

(OPPOSITE PAGE) *Nestled beneath a canopy of sycamore trees, Beaver Creek campground is the gateway to wilderness fishing and swimming holes.*
(ABOVE) *Towering Sunset Crater and the nearby Indian ruins of Wupatki are easily accessible from Bonito campground northeast of Flagstaff.*

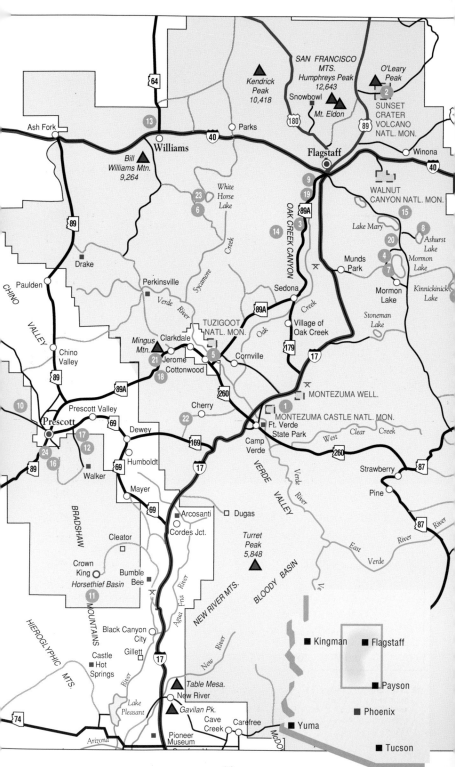

SAN FRANCISCO MTS.

Kendrick Peak 10,418

Humphreys Peak 12,643

Snowbowl

Mt. Eldon

O'Leary Peak

2

SUNSET CRATER VOLCANO NATL. MON.

Winona

Flagstaff

Parks

40

Williams

64

13

Ash Fork

Bill Williams Mtn. 9,264

White Horse Lake

23

6

WALNUT CANYON NATL. MON.

9

19

3

89A

15

Lake Mary

8

Ashurst Lake

14

20

Mormon Lake

4

89

Drake

Paulden

Perkinsville

Sycamore Creek

Verde River

Munds Park

7

Mormon Lake

Kinnikinick Lake

CHINO VALLEY

Sedona

89A

TUZIGOOT NATL. MON.

Oak Creek

Village of Oak Creek

Stoneman Lake

Chino Valley

Mingus Mtn.

Clarkdale

21

Jerome

18

Cottonwood

5

Cornville

179

17

OAK CREEK CANYON

89

MONTEZUMA WELL.

Cherry

22

MONTEZUMA CASTLE NATL. MON.

1

Ft. Verde State Park

10

Prescott Valley

69

Dewey

260

Camp Verde

West Clear Creek

Prescott

17

89A

17

Humboldt

Walker

69

Strawberry

87

Pine

24

16

12

Mayer

69

VERDE VALLEY

Verde River

87

Arcosanti

Dugas

BRADSHAW

Cordes Jct.

Turret Peak 5,848

BLOODY BASIN

East Verde

River

Cleator

Crown King

Bumble Bee

Horsethief Basin

11

MOUNTAINS

Black Canyon City

Castle Hot Springs

Gillett

17

NEW RIVER MTS.

Agua Fria River

New River

Ve

■ Kingman

■ Flagstaff

■ Payson

HIEROGLYPHIC MTS.

74

Lake Pleasant

Table Mesa.

New River

Gavilan Pk.

Cave Creek

Carefree

Pioneer Museum

Arizona

McD

■ Phoenix

■ Yuma

■ Tucson

42

REGION 2 RECREATION SITES *Handicapped access ^ Tents only	APPROX. ELEVATION	SEASONS OF USE ■	DAYS - LIMIT	FEE	APPROX. NO. OF UNITS	TRAILER LIMIT (FT)	FACILITIES				CONTACT INFORMATION
							SAFE WATER	RV DUMP STATION	RESTROOMS	SHOWERS	
1 Beaver Creek	3800	All Yr.	7	●	13	22	●		●		NFS2D
2 Bonito	6900	Mar. Oct.	14	●	41	22	●		●		NFS2C
3 *Cave Springs	5400	Apr. Sep.	7	●	78	32	●		●	●	NFS2D
4 Dairy Springs	7000	May Oct.	14	●	27	35	●		●		NFS2B
5 *Dead Horse Ranch	3300	All Yr.	15	●	150	45	●	●	●	●	ASP5
6 *Dogtown Lake	7000	Apr. Oct.	14	●	51	35	●	●	●		NFS4C
7 Double Springs	7000	May Oct.	14	●	16	35	●		●		NFS2B
8 Forked Pine	7100	May Sep.	14	●	25	15	●		●		NFS2B
9 Fort Tuthill	7000	May Sep.	14	●	100	Call	●	●	●		CRP4A
10 Yavapai	5600	All Yr.	14	●	25	40	●		●		NFS5A
11 Hazlett Hollow	6000	May Oct.	14	●	15	32	●		●		NFS5A
12 *Hilltop	5700	Apr. Oct.	7	●	38	40	●		●		NFS5A
13 *Kaibab Lake	6800	May Oct.	14	●	63	35	●	●	●		NFS4C
14 Kinnikinick Lake	7000	May Sep.	14	●	18	22	●		●		NFS2B
15 Lake View	6900	May Sep.	14	●	30	26	●		●		NFS2B
16 Lower Wolf Creek	6000	May Oct.	14	●	20	40			●		NFS5A
17 Lynx Lake	5500	Apr. Oct.	7	●	39	40	●		●		NFS5A
18 Mingus Mountain	7700	May Oct.	14		24	22			●		NFS5B
19 *Pine Flat	5500	Mar. Sep.	7	●	58	32	●		●		NFS2D
20 *Pinegrove	6900	Apr. Oct.	14	●	46	30	●		●		NFS2B
21 *Potato Patch	7000	May Oct.	14	●	40	40	●		●		NFS5B
22 Powell Springs	5200	All Yr.	14		10	16			●		NFS5B
23 *White Horse Lake	6600	May Oct.	14	●	94	38	●	●	●		NFS4C
24 White Spar	5700	All Yr.	14	●	61	32	●		●		NFS5A

■ Dates are approximate. Check with managing agencies if you are planning a trip near the start or end of the season. Contact information is on pages 186-192, where management agencies are listed alphabetically. The first two or three letters in the code for each campground designate the agency. The number and letters following the initial letters designate regions or districts.

nyon entrance are the remains of Mayhew's Lodge, which urned in the 1970s. Game and Fish personnel stock rainbow trout weekly in Oak Creek during summer months. Other available species include brown and brook trout, and small-mouth bass.

④ **DAIRY SPRINGS** campground, situated on the northwest end of Mormon Lake, lies just a city block off FR 90 reached from Flagstaff via Forest Highway 3 (Lake Mary Road). Set on a slight hill among ponderosas and scattered Gambel oaks, the campground and its amphitheater suggest a city park. In fact, schools, churches, and other organizations use it regularly. Like

other sites throughout the region, Dairy Springs' name taps into Arizona's history. In 1877, about 80 members of the Mormon Church brought a hundred cows here and established a dairy. Although Mormon Lake is small compared to some of Arizona's giants, at 600 acres (when full) it is the largest body of water in Coconino County. Fishing in Mormon Lake can be iffy because of fluctuating water levels. Northern pike were stocked here years ago, and some are still waiting to be caught, maybe giants. Nearby are numerous good trout-fishing lakes, like Upper and Lower Lake Mary, Ashurst, Kinnikinick, and Stoneman (a natural lake). Check your map. Campers in this area also enjoy some of the more diverse, "knockout" scenery in the world. Also, see Double Springs campground (No. 7 in this chapter), located about a mile south of here.

⑤ Camp at **DEAD HORSE RANCH STATE PARK**, along the Verde River at Cottonwood, and you will discover one of the best-kept campground secrets in central Arizona. It comes with all the comforts of home — hookups, showers, dump station, etc. — and is extremely under-used. Delightful, tree-shaded trails meander streamside from here, and Dead Horse makes an excellent base from which to explore the Verde Valley. Just a hop, skip, and a jump away are the ruins of ancient Tuzigoot and Montezuma Castle national monuments, the lively mining ghost town of Jerome, the colorful red rock country of Sedona and Oak Creek Canyon, and the scenic Verde Valley Railroad that departs from nearby Clarkdale. My

personal best time to camp here is middle- to late autumn. As for fishing, the Verde is rated very good for channel and flathead catfish, particularly in this area. You may also hook sunfish, the occasional largemouth or smallmouth bass, perhaps even a rainbow trout that has made its way here from Oak Creek.

(OPOSITE PAGE) *Ice rims Mormon Lake southeast of Flagstaff on a winter day. Winter sports at Mormon Lake include cross-country skiing and snowmobiling.* (ABOVE) *Tuzigoot National Monument near Clarkdale preserves a 700-year-old Sinagua Indian ruin west of Dead Horse Ranch State Park.*

⑥ The name **DOGTOWN LAKE** campground conjures up a less-than-flattering image until you learn that it refers not to our canine companions, but to prairie dogs who had a "city" here before it was inundated. To get here, take South Fourth Street (also named Perkinsville Road and Forest Service Road 173) out of Williams for about 3.5 miles, then left (east) on FR 140 for another 3 miles, then left on FR 132 for three-quarters of a mile to the lake. This is ponderosa-pine and Gambel-oak country, accented with occasional grassy meadows. Watch for Rocky Mountain mule deer. Through openings in the trees to the northeast you'll glimpse 9,388-foot-high Sitgreaves Mountain. Capt. Lorenzo Sitgreaves surveyed a wagon road through this area in 1852. Mountain man Bill Williams had a nearby mountain named for him, too. He acquired considerable fame as a scout, guide, and hunter. Dogtown Lake contains cold- and warm-water fish — rainbow, brown, and cutthroat trout; crappie; sunfish; and channel catfish.

⑦ **DOUBLE SPRINGS** campground, on the west side of Mormon Lake, occupies a pleasant niche in the Coconino National Forest. It's about 5 miles in on FR 90 from its junction with Forest Highway 3. The campground is close to the road and near the tiny community of Mormon Lake, which has a store and restaurant. Also, see Dairy Springs campground (No. 4 in this chapter), about a mile north of here.

8 **FORKED PINE** campground, about 24 miles southeast of Flagstaff along paved Forest Highway 3 and cindered FR 82E, sits on the northeast shore of Ashurst Lake. If you'd like a campsite with a picture-postcard view of the San Francisco Peaks, this is it. The Peaks stand 12,643 feet above sea level and are the centerpiece for a volcanic field that spreads over 2,000 square miles of north-central Arizona, including this campground. Soil here is but a thin veneer over ancient lava beds. Ashurst Lake campground is on the southwest side of the lake, but Forked Pine is my choice.

9 **FORT TUTHILL** campground sits in a cool ponderosa flat south of Flagstaff off Interstate 17 (Exit 337) at an elevation approaching 7,000 feet. The site of a military encampment in 1928, it is named for Brig. Gen. Alexander MacKenzie Tuthill, a former commander of the Arizona National Guard. Summer in the Flagstaff area was accurately described, in part, in an 1887 article by newspaperman George Tinker: " . . . the [summer] days being warm, the nights cold, the air dry, the scenery cheerful, and the sunlight brilliant. The San Francisco

(ABOVE) *At 50 acres, Dogtown is the largest lake in the Williams area. Camping alongside Dogtown gets you close to great fishing as well as great wildlife watching with deer, elk, antelope, turkey, and bear roam the surrounding forests and meadows. The Grand Canyon is only a few hours' drive from here.*

Peaks attract weather, with July and August and sometimes into September being the rainy season. But regularly, after wild thunderstorms, the sun breaks forth and the skies can be decorated with dramatic rainbows."

⑩ YAVAPAI campground near Prescott is off Iron Springs Road 3 miles northwest of the Miller Valley/Iron Springs/ Willow Creek junction, then north (right) 4 miles on FR 374. Two disabled-accessible sites have electricity for demonstrated

need. Open year round, Yavapai's just 1.6 miles from Granite Basin Lake, at the base of Granite Mountain. Hike or bike the trails to the pond-like lake, set amidst immense boulders and fringed with trees and cattails. There's boating (no swimming) and fishing for largemouth bass, sunfish, and channel catfish. Horseback riding is allowed at nearby Cayuse Equestrian Day Use Area.

⑪ HAZLETT HOLLOW campground, high in the Bradshaw Mountains, is 11 tortuous (some might use the word "torturous") miles south of Crown King on FR 52. Just getting to Crown King can be an adventure. Still, the dirt-street "Old West" community has a couple of restaurants and a general store-service station with camper supplies. Because of their proximity to Phoenix, Hazlett Hollow and Crown King have become popular destinations for escapees from the Sonoran Desert's summer heat. From the Horsethief lookout tower, near the end of FR 52, you can see the lights of Phoenix, 40 airline miles away. In June, millions of ladybugs gather around the tower, completely blanketing tree trunks, brush, and rocks. Largemouth bass, sunfish, bluegills, and channel catfish wait at Horsethief Lake. Great fun on light tackle. One local says a largemouth bass taken from the lake weighed 5 pounds. If you need a challenge, take FR 52 north. It's known as the Senator Highway and bumps and

grinds 31 miles (the word "torturous" applies here, too) from Crown King into Prescott. Named for the abandoned Senator Mine, it is anything but a highway. Some folks consider nego-

tiating it a feat worthy of admiration and respect. Don't be intimidated. It's an all-afternoon scenic forest drive. You can travel it with two-wheel drive (fair weather only), but a high-clearance vehicle is essential in order to prevent puncturing an oil pan.

⑫ HILLTOP campground, southeast of Prescott, lies a mile south of Lynx Lake off Forest Service Road 197, also called the Walker Road. It's very similar to the campground located at the lake, but without the standard shore activity and store. John James Audubon would have been content here. During my visit with the camp host I learned about a Hilltop highlight — there are sufficient numbers and species of birds to keep almost any enthusiast satisfied, and hummingbirds buzz around by the dozens. Also, see Lynx Lake campground No. 17 in this chapter).

⑬ KAIBAB LAKE campground is surrounded by a park-like forest of ponderosa pine trees just west of of State Route 64 (which connects Williams and the Grand Canyon) about 4 miles north of Williams and Interstate 40. The paved loops may cause some to feel like they aren't really camping. Others consider how much dust it keeps out of their tents, and out of their food. The Forest Service has arranged it with conveniences to make campers comfortable, yet still provide an outdoor experience. With State Route 64 the main artery to the Grand Canyon, this is a popular place. The campgrounds at Grand Canyon (See Mather, Desert View, and Ten-X in Region 1) often fill during "the season," causing many visitors to back-

(OPPOSITE, TOP) *Small but lovely Granite Basin Lake north of Prescott reflects the imposing bulk of Granite Mountain.*
(ABOVE AND OPPOSITE BOTTOM) *Horsethief Basin Lake at the southern tip of the Bradshaw Mountains attracts thousands of ladybugs as well as campers.*

track to Kaibab Lake. The small lake contains rainbow trout, sunfish, largemouth bass, and channel catfish.

⑭ **KINNIKINICK LAKE** campground covers a wind swept flat where a mixture of twisted juniper trees and open landscape fashions a surrealistic appearance. From Flagstaff, take paved Forest Highway 3 (Lake Mary Road) south for 30 miles to Forest Road 125, go east for 4 miles to FR 82, and then southeast for 5.5 miles to the campground. If you drive early or late in the day, you might see elk, deer, or both. Kinnikinick is an Indian word for the bearberry bush. This name has been affixed to other natural features in this high country environs: a spring, a canyon, and a stock tank referred to locally as North Kinnikinick. Rainbow trout swim in this shallow, 120-acre lake, along with channel catfish and a few bullheads. Migrating waterfowl use it as a resting and feeding place. Coots are commonly seen at Kinnikinick Lake.

⑮ **LAKE VIEW** campground, located 16 miles southeast of Flagstaff on Forest Highway 3, provides a good view of Upper Lake Mary, and it's for tent campers only. Camp sites are situated on the wooded slope of Anderson Mesa, a region known for elk, deer, and antelope herds. Abert squirrels, a tassel-eared relative of the endangered Kaibab squirrel, abound here, too. Canada geese and many species of ducks paddle about Upper Lake Mary, and at least one bald eagle has been known to fish here. In warm months, boaters, water-skiers, and fishermen find a working compromise. In winter, determined fisher folk brave snow, ice, and cold for rainbow trout, sunfish, channel catfish, northern pike, striped bass, and walleyes. However, the Forest Service closes this highly desirable campground after the Labor Day weekend.

⑯ **LOWER WOLF CREEK** campground is best reached from Prescott. Just head south on Mount Vernon Street, which will become FR 52. About nine miles out of Prescott turn west (right) on FR 97. Watch closely, as it's easy to miss the turn. When I visited, there were numerous vacant campsites under towering ponderosas. The host told me, there just isn't any potable water. Some campers can't handle that, even though

there are many other camping amenities such as a general store (that sells bottled water), modern restrooms, table-bench units, paved loops, the sweet scent of pine, free firewood, stress-free, spaced-out campsites, hiking in nice, clean, wild country, largemouth bass and panfish at nearby Goldwater Lake, a couple of restaurants, even a saloon just a few miles away, and — get this — the bonus of camping for free.

⑰ LYNX LAKE campground, south of State Route 69, is reached easily on paved FR 197. The 50-acre impoundment and its associated campground are enormously popular. The name is carried over from Lynx Creek. The story has it that in 1883 one Sam Miller grabbed a "lynx" floating in the creek. Sam probably was thinking that the animal was drowned. It wasn't. Chances are Miller tangled with a bobcat, which is slightly smaller and less formidable than a lynx. Nevertheless, he had a lot to talk about with the boys back in camp. The campground sits back from the shore among ponderosa pines.

On the north side of the lake there's a fully stocked store. Fish species waiting in the cool water include rainbow trout, largemouth bass, crappie, sunfish, and channel catfish. And when not using your pan to fry fish, you might try panning for gold in nearby streams. Also, see Hilltop campground (No. 12 in this chapter).

(OPPOSITE) *Kinnickinick Lake's restrooms are disguised as cozy cabins.*
(TOP) *Wolf Creek campground nestles amid ponderosa pines south of Prescott.*
(ABOVE) *Lynx Lake, southeast of Prescott, is near several campgrounds and features a store and boat rental.*

⑱ MINGUS MOUNTAIN campground is reached by a drive of 7 uphill miles on State Route 89A from the resurrected ghost town of Jerome. Then turn left onto dirt FR 104 at the pass. Another 2.5 miles brings you to the campground at the end of the road. Any time you get above 7,000 feet in Arizona, you can expect ponderosa pines, and that's the setting here. You'll need to be self-contained, but there's a payback. And that payback is the view. While stretching in the morning sun and enjoying your first cup of coffee you can overlook the

Verde Valley and see for a hundred miles. This is also a very popular jumping-off place, literally, for hang gliders.

⑲ PINE FLAT campground, located about 13 miles north of Sedona on SR 89A, is the northernmost campground in the Oak Creek Canyon chain. The higher elevation and the additional coolness, of course, is the reason for the ponderosa pines, and the campground's name. The loops are paved and, appropriately, sprinkled with pine needles. Pine Flat is not really flat, but this is as close as flat gets in Oak Creek Canyon — especially in its upper reaches. The creek at this point is brook-size and any fish caught — rainbow and some brown trout — will be similarly small. But that's not why most people camp here. The call of the canyon keeps the campground full all season long.

⓴ PINEGROVE campground is 35 miles southeast of Flagstaff and about a quarter-mile west of Forest Highway 3 on FR 651. Immediately after turning off the highway, you cross Walnut Creek, which will probably be dry or just a trickle. But thanks to this insignificant-appearing stream, there are the impoundments of Upper and Lower Lake Mary, where rainbow trout, panfish, northern pike, and walleye wait for anglers. The campground setting matches its name, Pinegrove, and it's one of the nicest mid-size Forest Service facilities in the state. The

wide-spaced sites are laid out well with convenient back-in or pull-through parking. Once set up you might enjoy exploring the region's back roads looking for deer and elk, or maybe just putting up your feet and relaxing around the campfire.

㉑ POTATO PATCH campground, 7 miles uphill on State Route 89A out of Jerome, rests in a hollow among the ponderosas on prime federal property. In addition to hiking trails and scenery, Potato Patch is a great place to think about and look at geology. (There's some rock hound in many of us.)

(OPPOSITE) *Mingus Mountain campground overlooks the Verde Valley and the red rock country of Sedona to the north and east.*
(ABOVE) *The oaks of upper Oak Creek Canyon surround Pine Flat campground north of Sedona.*

Between the boundary of Prescott National Forest to the west and Jerome to the east, you pass through Precambrian and Paleozoic rocks dating hundreds of millions to more than a billion years ago. On the northeast slope of these hills hangs Jerome, where Morris Andrew Ruffner discovered ore and filed a claim in 1876. Verde Valley mines have since produced $2 billion in copper, $60 million in silver and $50 million in gold.

22 **POWELL SPRINGS** campground, about 4 miles north of State Route 169 on FR 372, comes as a bit of a surprise. One minute you're driving through chaparral country and the next you're camped in a secluded pocket of ponderosa pines. This tiny campground is on the southeast slope of Mingus Mountain, and springs are abundant: Walnut, Bunker, Sunnybrook, Tunnel, Yellow Jacket, Black Rock, Slick Rock, Goat Peak, and Blue Monster, to name a few. Powell Springs was named for William Dempsey Powell, miner turned cattleman, who lived near here in 1875. For some spectacular views after you leave the campground, drive north through the clustering of homes called Cherry. About 11 miles later you'll be in the Verde Valley at State Route 260.

23 **WHITE HORSE LAKE** campground occupies the shoreline of this lovely lake 20 miles southeast of Williams. Take South Fourth Street for 9 miles and follow the signs to FR 110 and 109. Except for a few washboard places along FR 109, the all-weather, red-cinder road gets a good rating. This suggests that

the place receives a lot of local use. White Horse is popular. It supports a small resort with cabins for rent and a store with camping and fishing supplies, as well as boats for rent. It also makes an good base camp for exploring back roads and hiking, for example, Sycamore Wilderness. The average ponderosas are smaller here in the southern precincts of the Kaibab Forest, looking much like the lodgepole pines of Northwestern states.

The openness under their canopy makes spotting wildlife easy. Rocky Mountain mule deer commonly roam this high country. Some campers patrol the roads early or late in the day looking for animals browsing in the meadows. The campground spreads out on the west and south sides of the lake. On the east side of the lake, a prominent lava wall gives you an idea of what occurred here in the volcanic past. Marsh grass fringes the 40-acre lake and coots put on their usual ruffian show while several species of ducks quietly paddle about. A small boat is helpful for fishing, but some fisher folk do well from shore. Rainbow trout swim here, along with sunfish and channel catfish.

(OPPOSITE) *The resurrected ghost town of Jerome climbs Cleopatra Hill east of Potato Patch and Mingus campgrounds.*
(ABOVE) *White Horse Lake campground, south of Williams, is a fine fishing camp and base for exploring the upper reaches of the rugged Sycamore Canyon Wilderness.*

		Ashurst Lake	Wet Beaver Creek	Cataract Lake	Clear Creek (West)	Dead Horse Lake	Dogtown Reservoir	Goldwater Lake	Granite Basin Lake	Horsethief Lake
FACILITIES	BOAT RENTAL									
	MOTOR LIMITS	8hp		8hp				elec	elec	elec
	BOATS ALLOWED	●		●			●	●	●	●
	CAMP NEARBY	●	●	●		●	●		●	●
	STORE									
FISH SPECIES	BULLHEAD								●	
	WALLEYE									
	NORTHERN PIKE									
	CATFISH (Flathead)									
	CATFISH (Channel)	●		●		●	●	●	●	●
	SUNFISH			●		●	●	●	●	●
	CRAPPIE			●			●	●	●	
	STRIPED BASS									
	WHITE BASS									
	SM.MOUTH BASS		●		●					
	LG.MOUTH BASS			●		●		●	●	●
	CUTTHROAT						●			
	GRAYLING									
	BROOK									
	NATIVE									
	BROWN		●	●	●		●			
	RAINBOW	●	●	●	●	●	●			
	FLY & LURE ONLY									
	ELEVATION	7100	5000	6800	4870	3400	7070	5990	5600	6000
	AVERAGE DEPTH (IN FEET)	12		12		10	15	10	6	10
	AVERAGE ACREAGE	229		35		4	50	25	5	2

REGION 2 FISHING

Lake	Size (acres)	Depth	Elevation	Motor	C1	C2	C3	C4	C5	C6	C7	C8	C9	C10	C11	C12	C13	C14	C15	C16	C17
J.D. Dam Lake	6	6	6460	elec		●	●													●	●
Kaibab Lake	45	37	6790	8hp		●	●						●	●						●	
Kinnikinick Lake	126	22	7040	8hp		●	●		●				●							●	
Lake Mary (Lower)	100	12	6850		●	●	●	●		●	●		●							●	
Lake Mary (Upper)	600	38	6895			●	●			●	●		●	●		●		●		●	
Long Lake	268	25	6700			●	●		●	●	●		●	●				●		●	
Lynx Lake	55	40	5530	elec		●	●	●	●		●		●	●	●			●		●	
Mormon Lake	600	10	7100			●	●	●													
Oak Creek			3000-5900				●	●				●	●			●		●	●	●	
Oak Creek (West Fork)			5500																●	●	
Pecks Lake	70	5	3300			●	●			●			●	●	●			●			

57

REGION 2 FISHING

		Stehr Lake	Stoneman Lake	Verde River (Upper)	Watson Lake	White Horse Lake
FACILITIES	BOAT RENTAL				●	●
	MOTOR LIMITS	elec	elec			elec
	BOATS ALLOWED	●	●	●	●	●
	CAMP NEARBY	●	●	●	●	●
	STORE			●		●
FISH SPECIES	BULLHEAD					
	WALLEYE			●		
	NORTHERN PIKE		●			
	CATFISH (Flathead)			●		
	CATFISH (Channel)	●		●	●	●
	SUNFISH	●		●	●	●
	CRAPPIE				●	
	STRIPED BASS					
	WHITE BASS					
	SM.MOUTH BASS			●		
	LG.MOUTH BASS	●		●	●	
	CUTTHROAT					
	GRAYLING					
	BROOK					
	NATIVE					
	BROWN					
	RAINBOW			●		●
	FLY & LURE ONLY					
	ELEVATION	4500	6178	2900-5500	5100	6560
	AVERAGE DEPTH (IN FEET)	10	10		50	15
	AVERAGE ACREAGE	5	170		70	35

24 **WHITE SPAR** campground, about 3 miles southwest of Prescott and adjacent to State Route 89, is divided into two levels in the hilly, ponderosa pine landscape. Before construction of Interstate 17, State Route 89 was the shortest connection between the warm desert around Phoenix and cool northerly points like Prescott, Williams, and Flagstaff. The road, called "The White Spar," was dreaded because of its many mountain twists, but today it rates as a scenic drive.

(ABOVE) *Fishing from an inflatable tube allows this Arizona angler to get closer to the fish without the expense and inconvenience of hauling a boat.*

MOGOLLON RIM AREA
REGION 3
CAMPGROUNDS

No place in Arizona is more popular with campers than the Mogollon Rim. This forested escarpment at an elevation hovering around 7,000 feet is called simply "the Rim" by most locals and runs diagonally — northwest to southeast — across much of Arizona and into New Mexico.

Scientific studies show that temperature decreases by 3.5 degrees Fahrenheit with every 1,000-foot gain in elevation. Such a temperature drop is the equivalent of moving 300 miles toward the North Pole. With the Rim 6,000 feet higher than metropolitan Phoenix but just 100 miles away, an hour-and-a-half drive is — as far as temperature is concerned — the equivalent of traveling 1,800 miles north, which would put you somewhere near Yellow Knife, in Canada's Northwest Territories. Needless to say, the summer heat-suffering populace regularly makes the short trip to this cool land of conifers.

Small streams cascade southerly below the Rim. Above it, lakes dot the Colorado Plateau. The Arizona Game and Fish Department and the Apache-Sitgreaves, Coconino, and Tonto national forests have collaborated to provide extraordinary recreational opportunities. Lakes and streams are fish-filled, and elk, deer, turkey, bear and other wildlife are plentiful.

(OPPOSITE) *Atop the Mogollon Rim northeast of Strawberry, rainbow and brown trout swim in the waters of Blue Ridge Reservoir, which fill a steep-sided canyon.*

(ABOVE) *This awe-inspiring view of Tonto Basin is from the brink of the Mogollon Rim. Forest Road 300, a well-maintained gravel track through the ponderosa pines, parallels the edge of the Rim from State Route 260 near Woods Canyon Lake west to State Route 87 north of Strawberry.*

For just a touch of something different, the northern part of Region 3 includes a bit of the Painted Desert, the prehistoric Indian ruins of Homolovi Ruins State Park, and lastly, 20 miles southwest of Winslow, Meteor Crater, a visitor from outer space that left a calling card 570 feet deep and nearly a mile across.

① AIRPLANE FLAT is one of those places the Forest Service refers to as "dispersed camping," so be self-contained. It is rumored that the site got its name from a crash that occurred near here in the distant past, but nobody seems to know exactly where or when. The set-

ting, amid ponderosa pines at an elevation of about 6,600 feet, is pleasant. Canyon Creek is down the road less than a half-mile (fly- and lure-fishing only) and Canyon Creek Fish Hatchery is a very short distance upstream. To get to Airplane Flat, go southeast from State Route 260 on Forest Service Road 512 for about 3 miles, then turn east (left) on FR 33 for a little more than 4 steep, twisting miles.

② ASPEN and **③** SPILLWAY, with their paved loops, RV dump stations, hookups, and the nearby store and marina at Woods Canyon Lake, could give campers a feeling of being "downtown" (camp-style). Although several other camp-grounds are nearby, these two are the favorites. Thanks to thoughtfully located and amply spaced settings, you never lose the feeling of the great outdoors. Fifty-acre Woods Canyon Lake was the first man-made impoundment on the Rim. Although there is a lot of pressure on the lake, these popular waters are regularly stocked with catchable-size rainbow trout. Boats can be rented, but most fisher folk prefer to work from the shoreline. The campgrounds are next to Woods Canyon Lake. From State Route 260 about 25 miles west of Heber, take Forest Service Road 300 (across from the Rim Visitor Information Center) for about 5 miles and follow the signs. Casual hikers will enjoy the Rim Lakes Vista Trail, which includes a quarter-mile paved handicapped-access section, traverses the very edge of the Mogollon Rim.

④ BEAR CANYON LAKE offers a dispersed camp area where you'll find nearly level spots (near as they get around here) scattered among spruce, pine, and aspen trees. Restrooms are nearby at the lake, but otherwise be self-contained. There are no water or tables, but there also is no fee. Park anywhere you want — keeping in mind camping etiquette and the privacy of other campers. For some time, there's been a trend by state and

federal agencies to keep campgrounds away from fishing waters because of pollution and noise that go with them. This campground was one of Arizona's first attempts to achieve those goals. It was successful, yet the lake's paved parking area is only a quarter-mile away. Expect to catch rainbow trout and the distinctive grayling. Note: no bait fishing allowed, just lures or artificial flies. Getting here requires a little back-road driving. From the Woods Canyon Lake turnoff at State Route 260, go west on FR 300 about 12 miles to FR 89, then north (right) 3 miles to the lake and camp. The lake is about a quarter mile by foot trail from the camping area.

(OPPOSITE) *A young elk keeps a wary eye on intruders in the forest. Herds of American elk, or wapiti, roam Arizona's Rim country and White Mountains.* (ABOVE) *Woods Canyon Lake, the most popular Rim reservoir, features two campgrounds, a store, and boat rentals.*

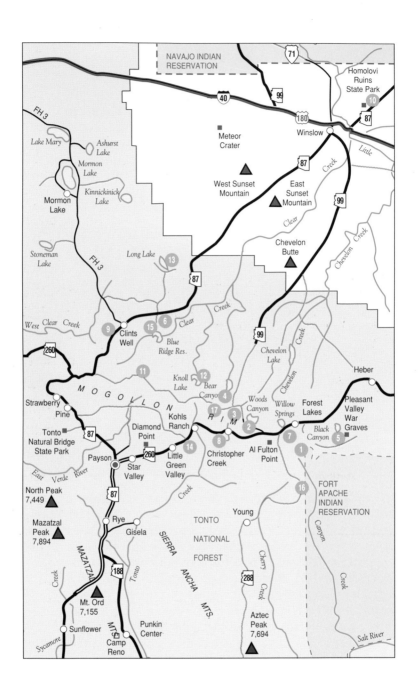

REGION 3 RECREATION SITES (D Dispersed Camping / *Handicapped access / ^ Tents only)	APPROX. ELEVATION	SEASONS OF USE ■	DAYS - LIMIT	FEE	APPROX. NO. OF UNITS	TRAILER LIMIT (FT.)	SAFE WATER	RV DUMP STATION	RESTROOMS	SHOWERS	CONTACT INFORMATION ■
1 Airplane Flat	6600	Apr. Nov.	14		D	16			●		NFS6E
2 Aspen	7600	May Oct.	14	●	136	Call	●	●	●		NFS1B
3 Spillway	7500	May Sep	14	●	26	16	●	●	●		NFS1B
4 Bear Canyon Lake	7600	May Oct.	14		D				●		NFS1B
5 Black Canyon Rim	7600	May Sep.	14	●	21	16	●		●		NFS1B
6 Blue Ridge	7200	May Oct.	14	●	10	32	●		●		NFS2A
7 *Canyon Point	7700	May Oct.	14	●	100	32	●	●	●	●	NFS1B
8 Christopher Creek	5600	Apr. Oct.	14	●	43	40	●		●		NFS6D
9 Clints Well	7000	May Nov.	14		7	22			●		NFS2A
10 Homolovi	5000	All Yr.	15	●	53	45	●	●	●	●	ASP6
11 Kehl Springs	7500	All Yr.	14		8	22			●		NFS2A
12 Knoll Lake	7300	May Sep.	14	●	33	22	●		●		NFS2A
13 Long Lake	6700	May Sep.	14		D						NFS2A
14 Ponderosa	5600	All Yr.	14	●	61	22	●	●	●		NFS6D
15 Rock Crossing	7500	May Sep.	14	●	35	32	●		●		NFS2A
16 Valentine Ridge	6600	Apr. Nov.	14		10	16			●		NFS6E
17 FR 9350	7600	May Sep.	14		D						NFS1B

■ Kingman   ■ Flagstaff

■ Payson

■ Phoenix

■ Yuma

■ Tucson

■ Dates are approximate. Check with managing agencies if you are planning a trip near the start or end of the season. Contact information is on pages 186-192, where management agencies are listed alphabetically. The first two or three letters in the code for each campground designate the agency. The number and letters following the initial letters designate regions or districts.

67

⑤ BLACK CANYON RIM campground, at times, has more hummingbirds than campers. Forest Service hosts regularly hang feeders to attract the birds, and the number of hummers earn convention status. Mule and white-tailed deer and elk frequent this part of the forest, occasionally ambling through camp. And it is highly likely that coyote songs will interrupt your evening fireside chatter. Of historical interest is the three-

quarter-mile trail to the grave site of James Stott, Jim Scott, and Billy Wilson. They were victims of a vigilante hanging during the Graham-Tewksbury feud (Pleasant Valley War) of the 1880s. For the fisher folk: head north about 3 miles on FR 86 and you're at Black Canyon Lake. Fish species here include rainbow trout. Tired of eating your own camp cooking? Continue north on FR 86 another 13 scenic miles to the mountain hamlets of Heber and Overgaard. You'll find restaurants, motels, gas stations, convenience markets, and the Heber District Office of the Apache-Sitgreaves National Forest. To get to the campground, drive about 2 miles east of Forest Lakes Estates on State Route 260, then south (right) for 2.5 miles on FR 300.

⑥ **BLUE RIDGE** campground rests in a sylvan pocket a mile or so southwest of the Blue Ridge Ranger Station off State Route 87, then another mile south (left) on Forest Service Route 138. The name is derived from the ridge that separates the campground from the lake of the same name. The story goes that when seen from the ridge top, the afternoon haze supposedly has a distinct bluish cast. Campers regularly report seeing elk, deer, bear, and eagles. There are restrooms, water, and table-bench units with fire rings and grills. Hikers and mountain bikers have access to nearby trails in the Coconino National Forest. Blue Ridge Reservoir, a narrow and winding trout lake with a boat ramp, is a few miles away off FR 751. For me, however, Blue Ridge's

main attraction is a contentment that pervades this campground, a pleasant feeling of just being here amidst solitude.

(OPPOSITE) *Black Canyon Lake, east of Overgaard, is a dependable trout lake, and the forest around it is filled with the history of the Pleasant Valley War.*
(ABOVE) *Young anglers explore Blue Ridge Reservoir by raft. Because of the steepness of the shore, a boat is almost a necessity when fishing here.*

⑦ CANYON POINT, a campground with water, paved loops, table-bench units, fire pits, restrooms, showers, and a dump station, most importantly has been well-designed to retain a feeling for the forest. And if you'd like to take a stroll in the woods, the easy three-quarter-mile (one-way) Sinkhole Hiking Trail starts on the "B" loop. A sinkhole is caused when rainwater seeps through cracks in the surface rock and dissolves underlying limestone, forming a small cavern. As the cavern grows larger, the roof collapses or "sinks." Walking into this 50-foot-deep sinkhole is like stepping back in time to a forest primeval. Canyon Point is 2 miles west of Forest Lakes Estates along the south side of State Route 260.

⑧ CHRISTOPHER CREEK campground is just west of the community of the same name along State Route 260 east of Milepost 271. It includes a group recreation site (reservations required) for no more than 25 people and seven vehicles. The

camp is situated below the Mogollon Rim, the abrupt southern edge of the Colorado Plateau, among red-barked ponderosa pines. Unlike so many campgrounds which are being moved away from water, this camp has Christopher Creek running right through the middle of it. This is one place where you can literally step out of your tent or RV and wet a line. The creek is stocked regularly with rainbows and fishing is good. Most catches are pan-size. The area is named for Frenchman Isadore Christopher, an early settler in these parts. It is said that Apache Indians swooped down on his cabin, burning parts of it to the ground. Issy was elsewhere at the time, but in an out-building he had a skinned bear, which was burned beyond recognition. Federal troops saw the smoke and hurried to the scene. They mistook the bear's carcass for Isadore's body and subsequently gave it a moving and dignified funeral. Despite property loss, Christopher chuckled at the events.

(OPPOSITE) *At Christopher Creek campground you can camp right on the bank and let the sound of running water lull you to sleep at night.*
(ABOVE) *The painted lady is an often seen butterfly in Arizona's high country.*

9 CLINTS WELL is a small campground tucked among giant ponderosas along Forest Highway 3 (the Happy Jack Highway) not far north of the junction with State Route 87. The site is named for Clint Wingfield, a storekeeper murdered in 1869 by notorious bandit Black Jack Ketchum, who was captured later for other nefarious acts, tried, and hanged. (Just as an aside —

"Happy Jack," the Coconino National Forest service camp 15 miles up the road, has nothing to do with Black Jack Ketchum. It was named by a Forest Service supervisor from Happy Jack, Montana.) About 10 miles south is Blue Ridge Reservoir, an impoundment on East Clear Creek. We're talking sizable rainbow and brown trout here.

10 HOMOLOVI RUINS STATE PARK combines the ancient with the modern. Campers can explore prehistoric ruins or venture on day trips throughout Arizona's north country. The campground has all you could want, including showers, dump station, and RV hookups, set against high desert grassland about 3 miles northeast of Winslow. Boating and fishing await you at the Clear Creek Reservoir, about 6 miles southeast of Winslow via State Routes 87 and 99. Homolovi means "place of little hills" in

Hopi, and the ruined walls and broken pottery are eloquent testimony of the Ancestural Puebloan culture, or *Hisat'sinom* in Hopi. Every June and July, archaeologists and volunteers search these wind-blown ruins for new insights into the Puebloans. Hopi clan elders, from their mesas 65 miles north, still make pilgrimages here, honoring their ancestors, who built this 1,000-room pueblo between A.D. 1250 and 1400. Homolovi is open 365 days a year, but winter winds on the Colorado Plateau are chilly. From Flagstaff, take Interstate 40 east to Exit 257 and go north on State Route 87, following the park signs.

⑪ KEHL SPRINGS campground is about 10 miles north of the mountain community of Strawberry, via State Route 87, then 7 miles east on Forest Route 300, usually referred to as the Rim Road. Another name for FR 300 is the Gen. George Crook Trail, after the famous general whose troops fought the Apaches that terrorized settlers in the area. General Crook's young soldiers in the 1870s built a wagon road linking across the rugged Rim linking Prescott and Fort Apache to facilitate their pursuit of the Indians. To mark the trail, the soldiers blazed the trees. Some of the blazes are still visible today more than a century later. As part of a bicentennial project in 1976,

Boy Scouts marked trees along the original wagon road with yellow chevrons.

En route to Kehl Springs the Rim Road winds through stands of ponderosa pine, Engelmann spruce, Douglas fir, and quaking aspen. You'll bisect fern-filled canyons along the way, and hit 8,000-feet elevation as you pass the road to Baker Butte fire look-out. While Kehl Springs is tiny, it is also one of the most enchanting campgrounds you'll ever visit. It is situated in a grassy meadow guarded by a split-rail fence, with an easy half-mile walk to the edge of the Mogollon Rim. Frequent comments about the view from the Rim include, "I feel like I'm standing on the edge of the world." There is no reliable spring at Kehl Springs, but an intermittent stream flows past the campground and the host says elk are regular visitors. This is good base from which to explore some of the many roads and trails threading the Coconino National Forest.

(OPPOSITE, TOP) *Blue Ridge Reservoir is the closest fishing to Clints Well.*
(OPPOSITE, BOTTOM) *Homolovi, "place of little hills" in the Hopi Indian language, is where the ancestors of the Hopi built an extensive settlement on the bluffs above the Little Colorado River 700 years ago.*
(ABOVE) *Kehl Springs, atop the Rim, was a stop on the General Crook Trail.*

⑫ KNOLL LAKE campground is hard to get to, but worth the trip. No matter how you approach it, it's a long, washboardy drive on Forest Route 300, then about 4 miles north on FR 295E to the lakeside camp. It is situated on the side of a ridge amid spruce, ponderosa, and aspen (which gives you an idea of the elevation). The camp sits slightly away from the lake, but believe me, you won't mind! Everything has been well-thought out for campers and fisher folk, including water. Caution: you better not forget your hamburger or tackle box, because it's a l-o-n-g way back to a store. The lake, created by putting a plug

in Leonard Canyon, is a 75-acre gem built by the Arizona Game and Fish Department in collaboration with the Forest Service. Fishing here is mainly for rainbow trout, and a boat and electric motor are helpful in catching them.

⑬ LONG LAKE offers no amenities except for relatively un-crowded camping among the pines and fine fishing almost on your doorstep. Dispersed campsites around the 270-acre lake are available on a first-come, first-served basis. Check with the vol-unteer camp host for the latest fishing information on catfish, walleye, pike, and trout. A good day's fishing here will yield qual-ity-size fish but probably not a mess of them. Soldier and Soldier Annex lakes are nearby. Take FR211 either from Forest Service Highway 3 (Lake Mary Road) on the west or from State route 87 on the east. At FR82, turn north and drive about 20 miles. Be alert for deer, elk, and antelope.

(OPPOSITE) *The stark beauty of granite outcroppings contrasts with the waters of Clear Creek Reservoir at Winslow's McHood Park, south of Homolovi Ruins State Park.*
(ABOVE) *Bring a small boat to Knoll Lake for the fishing, and picnic on the island that gives the lake its name.*

🄮 **PONDEROSA** campground, 15 miles east of Payson along State Route 260, may be the most appropriately named campground in the area. It lies within the largest stand of ponderosa pines in the world. These trees grow to over 100 feet high and can live as long as 350 years. Pick out an old red-barked giant for yourself. Put your nose right up to the bark and smell it. Ponderosas emit a wonderful vanilla-like fragrance that has been defined as "spiritual nourishment." Now sit on the ground, lean against the trunk, close your eyes, and listen. Naturalist John Muir once said "Of all the pines, this one gives forth the finest music to the winds." You will arise refreshed, and isn't that what camping is all about?

🄯 **ROCK CROSSING** campground sits in a pocket of ponderosas about 4 miles south of the Blue Ridge Ranger Station on State Route 87, then 3.5 miles east via FR 751 and 751A (sometimes called Blue Ridge Reservoir Road). About a mile beyond the campground an overlook provides a view of the reservoir. Zigzag down the hill to lake level and you'll suddenly find yourself beside the vaulted bulk of the concrete dam. The canyon is dramatically scenic, but the steep-sided walls tend to limit access. The V-shaped reservoir is about 8 miles long, making a boat essential for good fishing coverage. Look for rainbows. Four miles or so up the Clear Creek arm, just beyond the end of the lake and near the top of the canyon's south rim, is a plaque commemorating the Battle of Big Dry Wash. It was in this vicinity in 1882 that U.S. troops clashed with renegade Apaches in what turned out to be the last major battle of the Arizona Indian Wars.

⑯ VALENTINE RIDGE is a small, inviting campground below the Mogollon Rim. Table-bench units are arranged among the ponderosa, but the hillside setting is not suitable for trailers more than 16 feet long. The reason you want to spend time here is the campground's proximity to trout in Canyon Creek (about 1.5 miles away). This is quality fishing in a quality setting. Tiny Canyon Creek meanders for several miles through a

lush mountain meadow. Regulations limit it to fly and lure fishing only. An Arizona Game & Fish Department fish hatchery is located just upstream from the campground. Bring your all-terrain mountain bike: A 9-mile loop starts at the campground. Valentine Ridge is about 6 miles south of State Route 260 on FR 512 (the Young Road), then east on FR 188 about

(OPPOSITE) *Ponderosa campground off State Route 260 below the Rim is set amid an impressive stand of the pines for which it is named.*
(ABOVE) *While fly fishing along Canyon Creek below the Mogollon Rim you may think you're in Idaho or Montana.*

2 miles to the campground. Campground full? If you're self-contained, Valentine Canyon dispersed camping area is another three-quarters of a mile downhill on FR188.

🔢 **FR 9350 DISPERSED CAMPING AREA** could use a little more imagination in its name, but it pinpoints the locale. Take FR 300 and go 7 miles west from the junction with State Route 260. FR 9350, on your left, will dead-end in about 1.5 miles. But every eighth of a mile or so along the way, you'll see posts set back from the road in the forest with signs saying, "Camp Within 50 Feet." Some of these 40 or so units are only about 50 feet from the edge of the Mogollon Rim, presenting a view to enjoy at sunrise, sunset, or anytime. But you better not be afraid of heights, you better not be a sleepwalker, and you better be self-contained.

(OPPOSITE) *Views from the edge of the Mogollon Rim await campers at the dispersed campsites along Forest Road 9350, just south of the Rim Road, Forest Road 300.*
(ABOVE) *Below the Mogollon Rim, Tonto Creek is a popular hike destination.*

		Bear Canyon Lake	Black Canyon Lake	Blue Ridge Reservoir	Canyon Creek	Chevelon Canyon Lake	Chevelon Creek	Christopher Creek	Clear Creek (East)	Clear Creek Reservoir
FACILITIES	BOAT RENTAL									
	MOTOR LIMITS	elec	elec	8hp		8hp				
	BOATS ALLOWED	●	●	●		●			●	●
	CAMP NEARBY	●	●	●	●	●	●	●	●	●
	STORE							●		
FISH SPECIES	BULLHEAD									
	WALLEYE									
	NORTHERN PIKE									
	CATFISH (Flathead)									
	CATFISH (Channel)									●
	SUNFISH									●
	CRAPPIE									
	STRIPED BASS									
	WHITE BASS									
	SM.MOUTH BASS									
	LG.MOUTH BASS									●
	CUTTHROAT									
	GRAYLING	●								
	BROOK							●	●	
	NATIVE									
	BROWN					●	●	●	●	
	RAINBOW	●	●	●	●	●	●	●	●	●
	FLY & LURE ONLY					●	●			
	ELEVATION	7560	7100	6720	6100-6750	6380	6400-7000	5100-6600	5300-6800	4870
	AVERAGE DEPTH (IN FEET)	50	40	147		80				13
	AVERAGE ACREAGE	60	78	70		200				45

REGION 3 FISHING

Location	Elevation	Size	Motor
Haigler Creek	4000-5800		
Horton Creek	5400-6700		
Knoll Lake	7340	75	elec
Tonto Creek	4900-6900	50	
Verde River (East)	4400-6100	60	
Willow Springs Lake	7520	150	8hp
Woods Canyon Lake	7510	55	elec

WESTERN ARIZONA
REGION 4
CAMPGROUNDS

C amping in and getting a good look at this region, as in Region 1, means traveling long distances. Region 4 takes in more than 250 north-south miles along Arizona's western border, the Colorado River, from Lake Mead near Kingman in the north to Martinez Lake near Yuma in the south. Locally called the "Riviera," the region, like its Mediterranean namesake, has become an outdoor playground, not only for the rich and famous, but for hundreds of thousands of visitors each year who congregate along the entire length of the Lower Colorado for golden sun and blue water. The lower Colorado River also boasts Laughlin, Nevada, the gambling mecca across from Bullhead City, Arizona.

The Army Corps of Engineers and the Bureau of Reclamation have been active here, building five major dams: Hoover, Davis, Parker, Imperial, and Laguna, thereby impounding lakes Mead, Mohave, Havasu, Martinez, and Mittry, respectively. Taming the wild and muddy Colorado River has chagrined hard-core ecologists, but vastly pleased water-sports enthusiasts. Swimming, fishing, waterskiing, and

(OPPOSITE) *Houseboating, perhaps the ultimate in comfortable camping, takes you to great scenic locations such as Iceberg Canyon on Lake Mead. Obviously too warm for icebergs, it was the appearance of the rock formations that gave the canyon its name.*

(ABOVE) *Sun, sand, and the deep blue waters of Lake Mohave attract campers to Katherine Landing, north of Bullhead City.*

houseboating are extensive and popular nearly year-round.

The lower Colorado River Valley is part of the Pacific flyway, and abundant migratory birds use it in their north-south travels: Canada geese, ducks, mergansers, cormorants, and white pelicans, to name a few. The river runs through four national wildlife refuges — Topock, Havasu, Cibola, and

Imperial — all fine areas for bird lovers. A popular activity is canoeing quietly downstream from the Ehrenberg area to Martinez Lake, through Cibola and Imperial refuges. Expect to see considerable terrestrial wildlife species, too, including coyotes, raccoons, beavers, muskrats, and even desert bighorn sheep.

The Mohave Desert makes up most of Region 4 along the Colorado River but transitions into the Sonoran Desert as you travel east. Where the exact dividing line between these two deserts is, nobody can say for sure. You'll know you're in the Sonoran Desert when you camp at Organ Pipe Cactus National Monument, adjacent to the U.S. border with Mexico. The organ pipe and saguaro cacti are two identifying plants of the Sonoran Desert and grow nowhere else. If the wide variety of desert plants and animals is not enough to entertain you, keep in mind that much of Region 4 is rife with abandoned mines and the remains of mining towns. Keep your canteen and gas tank full, and have a good time.

① **ALAMO LAKE STATE PARK** campground overlooks the impoundment from a windy knoll covered with Mohave

Desert brush and cacti, and burros freely roam the rugged surroundings. In territorial days Alamo (Spanish for "cottonwood") was an important town and a crossing on the Bill Williams River. All are now submerged beneath the north end of the lake. Summer temperatures here get uncomfortably high, but fall, winter,

and spring are ideal. Alamo has long been recognized as a fish-ing hot spot for largemouth bass. You'll also find channel and flathead catfish, bullheads, tilapia (the African import), redear sunfish, bluegills, and carp. The lake also features a complete store and marina. Alamo is 41 paved miles north of Wenden off U.S. Route 60.

❷ BUCKSKIN MOUNTAIN STATE PARK sits amid the foothills of the Buckskin Mountains on the east bank of the lower Colorado River, 11 miles north of Parker. This deluxe campground has all the amenities, including paved pull-throughs for the folks with big rigs, and even an arcade for the kids. Before dams were built, cargo-laden steamboats plied the river that was so muddy it was described as "too thick to drink and too thin to plow." Today,

boating enthusiasts skim over water that is clear and cool. Pretty and park-like, Buckskin is neatly mani-cured with mown lawns and pampered mesquite and tamarisk. Two distinct groups of people make this a popular campground year-round. Fisher folk find it particularly enjoyable during winter months. Water enthusiasts with jet-powered boats and skis seem to prefer summer. But at all times, although the park is in Arizona, most of the license plates will be from California and elsewhere. Just north of Buckskin (and its associated River Island State Park) are the marshlands of Havasu National Wildlife Refuge. The area is noted for its variety of resident and seasonal waterfowl. These include great blue herons, greater and snowy egrets, black-crowned night herons, Canada geese, many kinds of ducks, an occasional eagle, and numerous other species. Fish species here include largemouth and striped bass, channel and flathead catfish, and panfish. Also, see River Island State Park (No. 11 in this chapter).

(OPPOSITE, TOP) *White pelicans gather on the big lakes formed by the impounded Colorado River that forms Arizona's western border.*
(OPPOSITE, BOTTOM) *Bass fishing is tops at Alamo Lake.*
(ABOVE) *Buckskin Mountain State Park is on the Colorado River near Parker.*

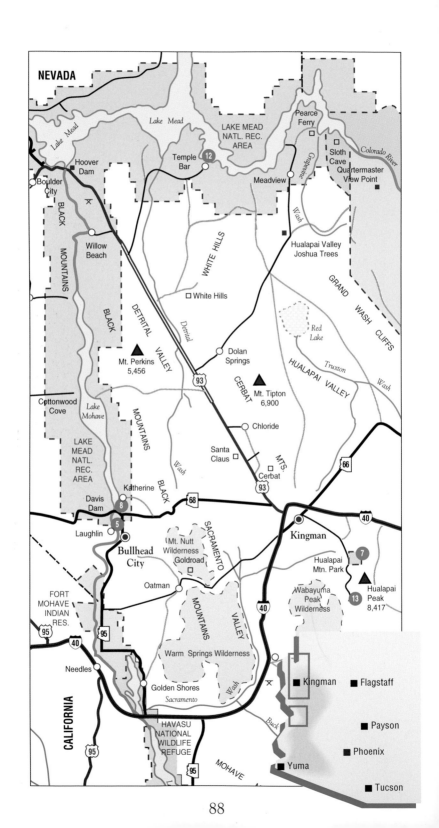

REGION 4 RECREATION SITES D Dispersed Camping *Handicapped access ^ Tents only	APPROX. ELEVATION	SEASONS OF USE ■	DAYS - LIMIT	FEE	APPROX. NO. OF UNITS	TRAILER LIMIT (FT)	FACILITIES SAFE WATER	RV DUMP STATION	RESTROOMS	SHOWERS	CONTACT INFORMATION ■
1 *Alamo Lake	1235	ALL YR.	15	●	250	Call	●	●	●	●	ASP1
2 *Buckskin Mountain	420	ALL YR.	15	●	68	Call	●	●	●	●	ASP2
3 *Burro Creek	1950	ALL YR.	14	●	25		●	●	●		BLM2
4 *Cattail Cove	450	ALL YR.	15	●	61	Call	●	●	●	●	ASP4
5 *Davis Camp	500	ALL YR.	14	●	180	Call	●	●	●	●	CRP2A
6 *Fishers Landing	350	ALL YR.	14	●	D		●	●	●	●	IJ1
7 *Hualapai Mountain Park	6500	ALL YR.	14	●	80	Call	●		●		CRP2B
8 *Katherine Landing	750	ALL YR.	30	●	165	45	●	●	●	●	NPS5A
9 *Organ Pipe Cactus N.M.	1700	ALL YR.	14	●	208	35	●		●		NPS7
10 *Painted Rock Petroglyph Site	700	ALL YR.	14	●	60	40			●		BLM3
11 *River Island	420	ALL YR.	15	●	37	Call	●	●	●	●	ASP12
12 *Temple Bar	1500	ALL YR.	30	●	153	45	●	●	●		NPS5B
13 Wild Cow Springs	6200	MAY OCT.	14	●	18	16			●		BLM2

■ See page 91

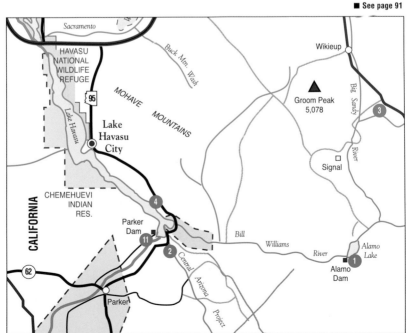

89

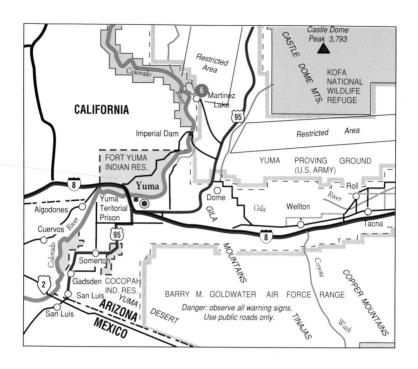

③ **BURRO CREEK** campground is just off U.S. Route 93 about 15 miles south of the community of Wikieup. In the mid-19th century, prospectors and miners searched the region for gold. Sometimes they lost their burros or turned them loose when they gave up in frustration. The creek was named in July 1869, when U.S. Army officers saw some of these feral burros watering there. Modern-day campers, especially in winter, hike up the stream seeking Nature's wonders. As for the gold, today Burro Creek is a regular stopover for tired casino-goers driving between Laughlin, Nevada, and Phoenix. Southeast of Burro Creek about 20 miles is the photogenic Joshua Forest Parkway. Although they may look like cacti, Joshua trees are members of the lily family. Check out Burro

Creek campground's "desert garden," a signed primer in familiarization of this terrain. Also, while exploring back roads in the nearby mountains, keep an eye out for bighorn sheep.

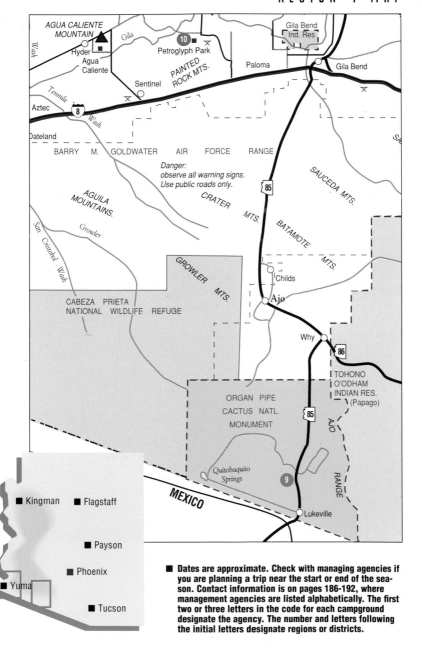

Danger: observe all warning signs. Use public roads only.

■ Dates are approximate. Check with managing agencies if you are planning a trip near the start or end of the season. Contact information is on pages 186-192, where management agencies are listed alphabetically. The first two or three letters in the code for each campground designate the agency. The number and letters following the initial letters designate regions or districts.

(OPPOSITE) *Two bridges span Burro Creek, the upper carries US Route 93, the lower, the road to Burro Creek campground.*

4 CATTAIL COVE campground is on the east shore of Lake Havasu, just off State Route 95. Campsites are close to one another, but for most it presents no problem in this well-maintained park. An alternate name for Cattail Cove might be "Smoke Tree," considering the quantity of them that appear on the landscape. Fifteen miles north is Lake Havasu City, old London Bridge, and the "English Village" at the bridge's base. With an excellent launching  ramp, boaters and fisher folk use Cattail as a jumping-off place to embrace Lake Havasu's water recreation. Though recognized primarily as a fine largemouth impoundment, other game-fish species include crappies, sunfish, channel catfish, and striped bass.

5 DAVIS CAMP, just north of Bullhead City and across the Colorado River from the casino town of Laughlin, Nevada, has grown from a primitive early-day campsite to a modern camping "community" with all the amenities — you can even buy a marriage license here. Upstream a few hundred yards stands the 140-foot-high concrete mass of Davis Dam, named for Arthur Powell Davis, Director of Reclamation 1914-1923. Although the main attractions are the casinos at Laughlin, fisher folk find this to be one of the hot spots on the Lower Colorado River for record-breaking striped bass. Hard-core striper fishermen use surf tackle to reach them. At Davis

Camp, however, more reasonable expectations include large-mouth bass, channel catfish, sunfish, and the occasional crappie.

⑥ FISHERS LANDING lies north of Yuma, about 10 miles west of State Route 95. You'll cross the austere Yuma Proving Grounds, and when Martinez Lake Road turns into a boat-launching ramp, you're there. Less than a city block away is Fisher's bar & grill and a marina. Locals call the primitive camping at Fisher's "boondocking," which is essentially the same as the Forest Service's "dispersed camping" — you get nothing but camp space under mesquite trees. You can pitch your tent or just spread your sleeping bag under the stars. However, you don't want to be here during summer unless you really like heat. Think 110° F. and more! But in cool weather, especially mid-winter, it's an outstanding place for active desert campers. Just 3 miles away, via dirt road, you'll find Imperial National Wildlife Refuge where 256 species of birds

have been recorded. It's not uncommon to see flocks of up to 300 white pelicans standing on a sandbar in the river or wheeling a thousand feet high on thermals. Bighorn sheep live in the adjacent Chocolate Mountains. Add to them raccoons, beavers, coyotes, and wild burros, and you have a good chance of spotting wildlife. Although not rated as a great fishery, the

(OPPOSITE, TOP) *Cattail Cove is a warm, sunny campground for fisherman in search of largemouth bass.*
(OPPOSITE, BOTTOM) *Record-breaking striped bass lure anglers to Davis Camp.*
(ABOVE) *Leisurly fishermen ply the waters at Imperial National Wildlife Refuge.*

Lower Colorado River contains a wide variety of species: large-mouth, smallmouth, and striped bass, crappie, bullheads, tilapia (an introduced African species), redear and green sunfish, and bluegills. Channel and flathead catfish also rate high here and some regularly tip the scales at 25 pounds. On weekends there's usually a lively band at one of the local establishments and, in a short time, the friendly folks make you feel like family.

7 **HUALAPAI MOUNTAIN PARK** is 12 miles up County Route 147 from downtown Kingman. At 8,417 feet high, Hualapai Peak can be seen from at least 40 miles away. The campground sits at the 6,500-foot elevation. The route up is steep, but is paved. Situated on the side of the mountain in sort of a "freestyle" scheme, the campsites are at many levels. Caution — neither the steep road nor small campsites are suit-

able for trailers or big motor homes. Dense stands of ponderosa pine line the loops, and Rocky Mountain mule deer and elk commonly browse the area. As with other of the state's islands-in-the-sky, some good hiking trails originate from the Hualapai Mountain Park area. For the rained-out camper, there are cabins nearby, along with a restaurant and lodge.

⑧ KATHERINE LANDING campground, on the eastern shore of Lake Mohave, is surrounded by pointed hills and thorny flora — prime Mohave Desert landscape. You could call this campground "Oleander City" for the shrubbery that serves as screens between units. Each unit also provides ample space to park your boat. Loops are paved and all amenities are nearby: restaurant, motel, store, marina, launching area, showers, boat berths, and houseboat rentals. Katherine Landing was named by miner J.S. Bagg in the early 1900s for his sister. Today it is noted as a largemouth bass fishery. Lake Mohave also provides rainbow trout, striped bass, channel and flathead catfish, and the occasional crappie. The campground lies six miles north of Bullhead City beyond the junction of State Routes 95 and 68.

(OPPOSITE) *The lodge and restaurant at Hualapai Mountain Park, east of Kingman, provide an alternative to camping.*
(ABOVE) *The geometric pattern of boat slips decorates Katherine Landing marina on Lake Mohave north of Bullhead City.*

⑨ ORGAN PIPE CACTUS NATIONAL MONUMENT campground, a mile off State Route 85, about 5 miles north of the U.S. and Mexico border, embraces the Sonoran Desert. Loops are paved and sites woven in among the natural flora. This park can truly be described as unique. In addition to organ pipe cacti, found only here and in adjacent Mexico, there are other rare plants such as the elephant tree. Organ Pipe is a top destination for winter visitors who like to anchor here with their RVs, stay their allotted 14 days, and return again when permitted for another 14 days. The monument has two unpaved but easily drivable scenic loops: Ajo Mountain Drive, 21 miles

around the east side of the monument, and Puerto Blanco Drive, 53 miles around the west side. Bring a picnic and plan on spending the day. Nowhere has nature presented more attractive slices of desert. On Puerto Blanco Drive [call to check its status], the tiny oasis of Quitobaquito Springs plays host to hundreds of species of birds. Here also swims the desert pupfish, a tiny aquatic creature that can exist in temperatures from near freezing to more than 100° F. During mornings and late afternoons, when shadows are long, the drives are at their best and offer fascinating vistas at every turn. That's also when you're most likely to see desert wildlife such as javelinas and coyotes. But even at mid-day, there are creatures on the move, like the rare and endangered Gila monsters, while overhead soar the seemingly ever-present red-tailed hawks. Strangely, these remarkable drives see very little traffic.

⑩ PAINTED ROCK PETROGLYPH SITE is about 12.5 miles west of Gila Bend. Exit Interstate 8 on Painted Rock Dam Road (Exit 102) and go north 10.7 miles on paved road to Rocky Point Road. The site is .6 mile west on Rocky Point Road. It is a quiet and restful place in winter, but uncomfortably hot during summer. (Winter temperatures can vary from freezing at night to 80° F. in daytime.) The main feature, and worth the trip even if you don't plan to camp there, is an acre of rocks – some boulders about 30 feet high – with hundreds of petroglyphs of birds, snakes, lizards, stick people, and abstract shapes. It is believed the glyphs were pecked into the dark

"desert varnish" surface of the stone first by the indigenous people of the Archaic Period (6,000 to 2,000 years ago) and on up to the Hohokam people of 2,000 to 600 years ago. From the mid-1850s until the outbreak of the Civil War, the Butterfield Stage passed these rocks several times a week on its southern route from St. Louis to San Francisco. Few places give a better idea of what desert travelers must have been concerned about a couple of hundred years ago. Bring your own water and wood for the campfire. You'll want to stay up and watch the stars, and the coyotes will help you stay awake.

⑪ RIVER ISLAND campground, about 13 miles north of Parker along State Route 95, is a unit of Buckskin Mountain State Park. The manicured lawn makes some people think they are about to camp in the front yard of some mansion. The site is nestled between a pair of volcanic cliffs on two sides, and between the highway and the Colorado River on the other sides, but that is as close as it comes to being an island. Choice riverfront units go to tenters. (Also see Buckskin Mountain.)

(OPPOSITE) *Organ Pipe Cactus National Monument is the epitome of pristine desert camping in the warm winter sun of southwestern Arizona.*
(ABOVE) *At Painted Rock Petroglyph Site you'll camp where ancient desert cultures gathered and left messages carved into sun-burnished stone.*

⑫ The shady **TEMPLE BAR** campground, landscaped with oleanders and eucalyptus, is almost inviting enough for permanent living. Located near the south shore of the Colorado River arm of Lake Mead, the campground is about 28 miles north along Detrital Wash from U.S. Route 93. En route to this campground you pass through a slice of the Mohave Desert decorated with ocotillos and Joshua trees. At least one pair of golden eagles has been known to hunt here and play on the thermals. The Temple Bar community has a restaurant, store, motel, and marina. Some people come here to rent a houseboat or pontoon boat (reservations required) and camp on the lakeshore. Others use the campground as a base camp and take boating day trips. Lake Mead, an easy stroll from the campground, is the largest capacity man-made reservoir in America.

There are hundreds of miles of shoreline for water-oriented recreationists. Fishermen find that Mead (named for Dr. Elwood Mead, commissioner of reclamation from 1924 to 1936) is primarily a largemouth lake, but you may pick up an occasional striped bass, channel catfish, and lots of panfish.

⑬ **WILD COW SPRINGS** sits in a pocket of Gambel oak and ponderosas on the southerly side of Hualapai Peak outside Kingman. Because the latter part of the drive is so rough, four-wheel-drive, high-clearance vehicles are preferred, and the rough section and tight mountain switchbacks make towing a trailer impossible. Go 13 uphill miles southeast of Kingman on County Route 147 (Hualapai Mountain Road), then go 4 miles south. Upon leaving County 147, you'll think you're just wandering about in the summer-home area of Pine Lake, but the route's signs are easy to follow. However, the road worsens at the turnoff , where it becomes an unpaved, single lane that is steep, rough, and narrow. Farther up the mountain, you still have to deal with mountain-road switchbacks. The road takes you winding around boulders and between ponderosa and oak trees. The going will be slow, but you'll enjoy the dramatic views of the Mohave Desert below and the Aquarius Mountains far to the east. The route invites you to cruise lazily along with the windows down so you can enjoy the cooler

mountain air. If you make the drive early or late in the day, you're almost guaranteed a deer sighting. Moreover, the Gambel's quail don't seem in much of a hurry to cross the road, either.

(OPPOSITE) *Temple Bar, the rock formation for which the settlement was named, rises majestically from Lake Mead.*
(ABOVE) *A dirt track winds its way through the scenic Hualapai Mountains to Wild Cow Springs campground.*

REGION 4 FISHING

		Lake Havasu	Cattail Cove	Crazy Horse	Main Marina Area	Windsor Beach	Alamo Lake	Bill Williams River	COLORADO RIVER — Buckskin Mountain State Park	Parker vicinity
FACILITIES	BOAT RENTAL	●	●		●		●			●
	MOTOR LIMITS									
	BOATS ALLOWED	●	●	●	●	●	●	●	●	●
	CAMP NEARBY	●	●	●		●	●	●	●	●
	STORE	●	●	●	●		●		●	●
FISH SPECIES	CARP						●	●		●
	SUNFISH (Bluegill)						●	●	●	●
	SUNFISH (Green)						●	●	●	●
	SUNFISH (Redear)	●	●	●	●	●	●	●	●	●
	TILAPIA						●			
	CATFISH (Flathead)	●	●	●	●	●	●	●		
	CATFISH (Channel)	●	●	●	●	●	●	●	●	●
	BULLHEAD	●	●	●	●	●	●	●		●
	CRAPPIE	●	●	●	●	●	●			●
	STRIPED BASS	●	●	●	●	●			●	●
	WHITE BASS									
	SM.MOUTH BASS									
	LG.MOUTH BASS	●	●	●	●	●	●	●	●	●
	CUTTHROAT									
	GRAYLING									
	BROOK									
	NATIVE									
	BROWN									
	RAINBOW	●								
	FLY & LURE ONLY									
	ELEVATION	480					1100	480	440	420
	AVERAGE DEPTH (IN FEET)	35					80		7	7
	AVERAGE ACREAGE	19,300					3500			

100

	Martinez Lake Marina	Fishers Landing	Imperial Oasis	Laguna Dam and above	Laguna Dam to Morelos	Mittry Lake	Gila River confluence eastward
	●	●	●				
	●	●	●	●	●	●	●
	●	●	●				
	●	●	●				
	●	●	●	●	●	●	●
	●	●	●	●	●	●	●
	●	●	●	●	●	●	●
	●	●	●	●	●	●	●
	●	●	●	●	●	●	●
	●	●	●	●	●	●	●
	●	●	●	●	●	●	●
	●	●	●	●	●	●	●
	●	●	●	●	●	●	●
	●	●	●	●	●	●	●
	●	●	●	●	●		●
	●	●	●				
	●	●	●	●	●	●	●
	1-10		1-10	1-10	1-10	500	0-4
						8	
	230	200	200	200	150	185	190

CENTRAL ARIZONA
REGION 5
CAMPGROUNDS

C amping in this region may require some mental adjustments. When you see the sign, "Tonto National Forest," there may be nothing but cacti behind it. Sure, there are trees out there: mesquite, ironwood, paloverde; and incredible things bloom in the spring. But some of the cacti, the saguaro in particular, are taller than the trees. If you insist on "standard" forest-type trees, take State Route 288 from Roosevelt Lake into the Sierra Anchas. It's an impressive drive. Still, the greater part of Region 5 is Sonoran Desert and sports some truly unique camping country.

But you don't have to be a Lawrence of Arabia to camp here. Literary giant Joseph Wood Krutch stood in the middle of this landscape and asked, "Where's the desert?" That's because the Sonoran is heavily vegetated as deserts go, and it is equally heavily populated with wildlife. Here thrive desert mule deer, coyotes, javelinas, jackrabbits, and roadrunners and quail, birds that would rather run than fly.

This is lake country, too. Lake Pleasant on the Agua Fria River; Horseshoe and Bartlett lakes on the Verde River; and Saguaro, Canyon, Apache, and Roosevelt lakes on the Salt

(OPPOSITE) *Fall, winter and spring camping, a luxury in most states, is a given in the the warm deserts of southern Arizona. Here a camper enjoys shoreline camping at Lake Pleasant, northwest of Phoenix.*

(ABOVE) *Cold above, warm below, elevation makes all the difference in temperature in Arizona. Snow frosts the 7,645-foot-high summit of the Four Peaks range northeast of Phoenix, while the Sonoran Desert below basks in warm sunshine.*

River, all within a few miles of the queen city of the desert, Phoenix. No, we're not talking mirages here; these reservoirs are frequently written up in national outdoor magazines for their exceptional fishing.

Think variety in this country and, in a short time, you might find "desert rat" is an affectionate description of yourself.

① **BURNT CORRAL** campground, on the upper end of Apache Lake, has been laid out among desert flora in a scenic pocket of Salt River Canyon. And while it has paved loops and modern toilets, the camp "feeling" is strong at this site. Gambel's quail are permanent residents, an occasional road-runner passes through, and numerous other species keep birders busy with their binoculars. Cottontail rabbits are common and campers may see coyotes in pursuit of them; you'll sure hear the coyotes at night. Even desert mule deer trip by, and sometimes a band of javelinas. The narrow lake is about 10 miles long and the shoreline is steep and rocky. All in all it's an attractive desert setting for camping and fishing. The sport fish that swim here are rainbow trout, largemouth and small-mouth bass, crappie, sunfish, channel and flathead catfish, and walleye. Of all the species, many locals find the feisty small-mouth to be the most interesting. A boat definitely increases your chances of success. To find Burnt Corral, take State Route 88 (the Apache Trail) from Apache Junction to Forest Service Road 183 (about 6 miles south of Roosevelt Dam) and drive a mile to the site on the south side of Apache Lake.

(OPPOSITE AND ABOVE) *Apache Lake, one of the four Salt River reservoirs east of metropolitan Phoenix, offers rugged desert canyon scenery, warm temperatures, and great bass fishing.*

REGION 5
RECREATION SITES
D Dispersed Camping
*Handicapped access
^ Tents only

	APPROX. ELEVATION	SEASONS OF USE ■	DAYS - LIMIT	FEE	APPROX. NO. OF UNITS	TRAILER LIMIT (FT)	FACILITIES: SAFE WATER	RV DUMP STATION	RESTROOMS	SHOWERS	CONTACT INFORMATION ■
1 *Burnt Corral	1900	ALL YR.	14	●	80	22	●		●		NFS6F
2 *Cholla Rec. Site	2200	ALL YR.	14	●	210	32	●	●	●	●	NFS6F
3 *Lost Dutchman Park	2000	ALL YR.	15	●	70	Call	●	●	●	●	ASP7
4 *McDowell Mtn. Park	2000	ALL YR.	14	●	75	Call	●	●	●	●	CRP1A
5 Pinal	7500	MAY OCT.	14		20	16	●		●		NFS6B
6 Rose Creek	5400	APR. NOV.	14		5	16			●		NFS6E
7 *Schoolhouse Rec. Site	2200	ALL YR.	14	●	210	32	●		●		NFS6F
8 Seven Springs	3400	ALL YR.	14	●	25	16	●		●		NFS6A
9 *Tortilla	1800	OCT. APR.	14	●	80	22	●		●		NFS6C
10 *Usery Mountain	2000	ALL YR.	14	●	75	Call	●	●	●	●	CRP1B
11 *White Tank	1500	ALL YR.	14	●	75	Call	●		●	●	CRP1C
12 *Windy Hill Rec. Site	2200	ALL YR.	14	●	350	32	●	●	●	●	NFS6F

■ Kingman ■ Flagstaff

■ Payson

■ Phoenix

■ Yuma

■ Tucson

■ Dates are approximate. Check with managing agencies if you are planning a trip near the start or end of the season. Contact information is on pages 186-192, where management agencies are listed alphabetically. The first two or three letters in the code for each campground designate the agency. The number and letters following the initial letters designate regions or districts.

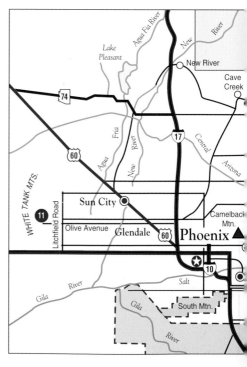

❷ CHOLLA RECREATION SITE, a solar-powered, have-everything campground, might remind you of a well-designed RV park. It's a place to spend the entire winter. Moreover, if the campground doesn't fill, they'll let you. From Cholla, the 360-degree view of central Arizona scenery is fantastic. Roosevelt Lake, of course, reflects the turquoise of the sky. The colorful Sierra Anchas, located to the east and to the west, include Four Peaks, among Arizona's most recognizable mountains. The site has playgrounds and barrier-free access to trails suitable for wheelchairs. Still, the big draw here is fishing. Roosevelt Lake is widely recognized as a largemouth bass lake. Other species are smallmouth bass, sunfish, channel and flathead catfish, and crappies. Cholla is about 6 miles north of Roosevelt Dam along State Route 188. From Mesa, take State Route 87 to SR 188, turn right and go 28 miles. From Globe, take 188 north from its junction with U.S. Route 60. Also, see Schoolhouse Point (No. 7) and Windy Hill (No. 12) in this chapter. On the opposite side of State Route 188, near the entrance to Cholla, is the Three Bar Wildlife Area. If you feel a need to see a javelina, slowly drive Forest Service Road 647 early or late in the day. No guarantees, but good possibilities of spotting a herd or other animals.

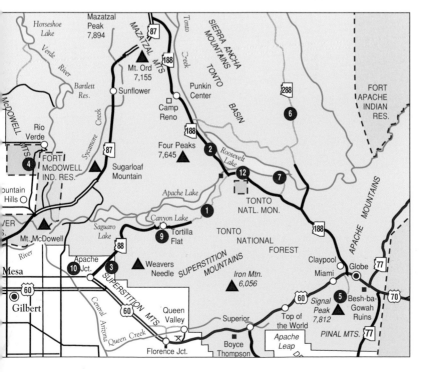

❸ LOST DUTCHMAN STATE PARK, about five miles northeast of Apache Junction along State Route 88, sits on a gentle slope of a region of Arizona that has captured the imagination of the world: the Superstition Mountains. Somewhere in the craggy volcanic lands above the park, legend says, hides the Lost Dutchman Gold Mine. Jacob Waltz, better known as "the Dutchman," started it all in 1871 when he staggered into Phoenix with some gold nuggets. Locals eventually deduced, likely incorrectly, that he had found them in the Superstition Mountains. After more than a hundred years of searching, no one has come forth with the riches. Most gold-seekers have focused on the area around Weaver's Needle, a striking volcanic pinnacle in the Superstition Wilderness. If you'd like, drive up State Route 88 a short distance to the formal view-

point and get a really good look at it. Lost Dutchman campground is in a natural setting of cacti and other Sonoran Desert plants. Animals that regularly visit the park include lizards, jackrabbits, coyotes, and desert mule deer. Park personnel classify the campground as "undeveloped," a term that may intimidate some campers. Others of us just see a lack of showers as part of the outdoor experience. Conveniences, if you really need them, are back down the road at Apache Junction, where stores, shops, restaurants, and motels are scattered along the highway.

④ **McDowell Mountain Park**, east of central Phoenix and about 5 miles north of Fountain Hills, appears to be more RV park than campground. But tenters and backpackers are welcome to throw down their bedrolls here, too. The setting is

ideal Sonoran Desert country. Though fenced in on three sides by civilization, the park still provides a quality outdoor experience. From its hilltop location you get commanding views of the desert, including Four Peaks. During winter, any snow that chances into this sun-drenched country usually collects first on Four Peaks. The scene

is so dramatically beautiful that even locals come out to stare in wonder. From Shea Boulevard, go north on Fountain Hills Boulevard, which merges into McDowell Mountain Road, which leads to the park. Or take Saguaro Boulevard from Shea to Fountain Hills Boulevard and turn right to McDowell Mountain Road.

(OPPOSITE) *The legendary Superstition Mountains form the scenic backdrop for Lost Dutchman State Park east of metropolitan Phoenix.*
(TOP) *Spring on the Sonoran Desert brings out the strawberry hedgehog blooms.*
(ABOVE) *Spectacular stands of saguaro cacti thrive at McDowell Mountain Park.*

5 PINAL campground is at the upper reaches of pine-topped Pinal Mountain, where Signal Peak, at 7,812 feet, once was part of a chain of heliograph stations that extended into Texas. Sending messages by reflected sunlight permitted the Army to communicate across hundreds of miles and helped lead to the capture of Geronimo. It's especially grand here in fall when aspens turn gold. The road can be exciting in places, one lane, steep, switchbacks, and sometimes nothing but sky on the outside shoulder. Caution: Only small RVs are recommended because of the road and restricted camp units. Spectacular views spread out just a few yards away from the campsite. Across from the junction of U.S. Route 60 and State Route 188 between Miami and Globe, head south on Forest Service Road 55 (Russell Road). After about 8 miles, turn right onto FR 651 and go about 10 miles to Pinal campground. From Globe, take Jess Hayes Road off U.S. 60 to the junction of Ice House Canyon (FR 112) and Sixshooter Canyon (FR 222) roads. Turn right and continue on 112 for 3 miles to the junction of FR55, bear left and continue to FR 651 and the campground.

6 ROSE CREEK campground is in the mountains high above Roosevelt Lake. Graveled and graded State Route 288 switchbacks up from the cactus lowlands around Roosevelt, granting astonishing views that would be considered for national-park status in most other states. At the campground, seemingly enchanted sycamores hover over the five compact units. Anyone from Ireland will be inclined to peep cautiously here and there in this shadowed green glen to catch a glimpse of one of the "wee folk." Brook-like Rose Creek tumbles through

(OPPOSITE) *Ridgeline after ridgeline recede to the horizon from the heights of the Pinal Mountains near Globe.*
(ABOVE) *Rose Creek trickles through a forest glade high in the Sierra Ancha Mountains northeast of Roosevelt Lake.*

thick vegetation that embraces sumac and wild grape. Sure now and Rose Creek may have curative powers. Tired and sweaty after climbing 3,000 feet out of the desert heat, I plunged my face into these limpid waters and felt immediately revived. Rose Creek country is bear country, too, but seeing one is almost as difficult as catching a glimpse of a leprechaun. The camp is a few hundred yards off State Route 288, and along very short FR 152.

7 SCHOOLHOUSE RECREATION SITE, like Cholla and Windy Hill sites, is a has-everything camping area on delta land where the Salt River flows into Roosevelt Lake. From here, you readily can reach the lake and the river and several miles of trails. Late on a winter afternoon the shadowed view of Four Peaks, the multicolored bluffs of the Sierra Anchas, and the reflected sky blue of the lake will knock your socks off.

Add to that marshlands to the east that at times are so heavily populated with waterfowl some people push the usual priority of fishing into second place. Wow! The site is well prepared for RVs but has tent-only sites as well. Schoolhouse is 11 miles south of historic Roosevelt Dam. From Mesa, take State Route 87 northeast to State Route 188; then right (southeast) for about 41 miles to Forest Service Road 447; then left (east) for 4 miles. From Globe, take SR188 north from U.S. 60 for about 20 miles to FR 447.

⑧ SEVEN SPRINGS, 20 miles north of Carefree on Forest Route 24 (Cave Creek Road), is surrounded by prime Sonoran Desert. But the oasis-like campground sits under a cooling canopy of sycamore and cottonwood trees. Combine this setting with its proximity to metro Phoenix and you have one very popular place to camp and hike — there are many trails

in the area, including one along a small creek cradled by sycamore trees. During autumn, hunters find it an ideal base from which to seek quail and javelina. FR 24's alternate I.D. is "Bloody Basin Road." The "bloody" recalls skirmishes the Apaches and U.S. Cavalry once had in the area. Any car can make the trip to Seven Springs. However,

driving the forest roads north of here falls under the category of "challenging." That is wild, open country and the roads are rough and rugged. A high-clearance vehicle is required, but four-wheel drive is preferred. Don't fool with Mother Nature! Be prepared.

(OPPOSITE) *The Four Peaks form a distinctive outline on the horizon seen from Schoolhouse Point on Lake Roosevelt.*
(TOP) *A desert mule deer warily eyes an intruder in his prickly pear cactus patch.*
(ABOVE) *Autumn paints the sycamores that shade Seven Springs campground.*

9 TORTILLA campground sits at Tortilla Flat, 18 paved but twisting miles up State Route 88 from Apache Junction. The portion of the drive along the southern shore of Canyon Lake is breathtaking, and the campground is not far behind the ridge at the lake's eastern end. This is another location at the edge of the Superstition Wilderness. Like Lost Dutchman State Park, the decor is prime Sonoran Desert, but this site is a bit more remote and Tortilla Creek tumbles by the base of the hill. Tortillas, as most already know, are a type of wonder-

ful flat bread used as the foundation of numerous savory Mexican dishes. Apparently somebody once thought the weathered bluff on the opposite side of the creek looked like a stack of tortillas, thus the name. Across the road from the campground is tiny Tortilla Flat restaurant and general store. It's a popular stop-and-stretch place along the Apache Trail for weekend and day-trip visitors from the Valley of the Sun.

10 USERY MOUNTAIN REGIONAL PARK, on the eastern edge of Mesa, Arizona's third largest city, is mostly an RV park. Nevertheless, the feeling of the desert is strong, and units are separated by lush vegetation — giant saguaros, prickly pear, and ocotillo, for example. In spring colorful wildflowers such as golden poppies, violet-colored owl clover, purple lupine, and yellow brittlebush blanket the mountain slopes. Beyond the park to the east, the mysterious Superstition Mountains appear to hang from under the sky. But immediately at hand is Usery Mountain, with mysteries of its own. Hike the trail to Wind Cave and discover a few. Usery Mountain and Park were named for King Usery, a rancher who ran cattle here in the 1870s and 80s. One way to reach Usery is to take U.S. Route 60 (Superstition Freeway) to the east side of Mesa. Exit at Ellsworth Road and go north six miles to the park entrance. (Ellsworth becomes Usery Pass Road.)

(OPPOSITE) *The Salt River, designated wild and scenic above Roosevelt Lake, becomes a torrent of white water during spring runoff.*
(ABOVE) *Tortilla Flat, a restaurant and store near Canyon Lake, serves as a welcome rest stop for many travelers along the beautiful but winding Apache Trail.*

⑪ WHITE TANK REGIONAL PARK is about 25 miles west of central Phoenix in the White Tank Mountains. Here, paved loops harboring campsites and day-use facilities wind in and out of a Sonoran Desert setting. On varying schedules, park rangers lead hikes to Hohokam petroglyphs, a waterfall (only after a rain), and other sites. Some tours are along barrier-free routes for youngsters, the elderly, and wheelchair-bound people. Star-gazers also enjoy the area. Call the park for details.

Although on weekends there may be considerable activity in the park's picnic areas and on the many White Tank trails, you can expect peace and quiet in the campground. Most of the time any noises you hear, outside of quail and the raucous cactus wrens, are occasional jets from Luke Air Force Base to the east. During daytime hours you'll be entertained by these "star wars" craft. From Interstate 17, take Loop 101 west to the Olive Avenue exit; then go west to the park. From Interstate 10 west of central Phoenix, take Loop 303 north to Olive Avenue. The park entrance gate is about 4 miles west of Loop 303.

⑫ WINDY HILL RECREATION SITE, as its name indicates, sits atop Windy Hill on the Salt River arm of Roosevelt Lake. Camp sites are located on paved loops extending along ridges dotted with desert vegetation. Conveniences include fire rings, barbecues, individual ramadas shading table-bench units, playgrounds and an amphitheater, a picnic-only area, and solar-heated showers. Along with Cholla Recreation Site (No. 2 in this chapter), Windy Hill ranks among the largest camping sites with solar power. Roosevelt Marina is about 2.5 miles east along State Route 188. Also, this was prehistoric Salado Indian Country. They used water from the Salt River for farming corn, beans, squash, and cotton. The Salado departed the area about 600 years ago, but some of their housing sites remain. Drop by Tonto National Monument, about a mile from here on the west side of SR188, and tour the cliff dwellings. From Mesa, take State Route 87 northeast to SR188; then southeast for about 37 miles to Forest Service Road 82; then left for 2 miles.

(ABOVE) *Depressions in light-colored rocks become water tanks, giving the White Tank Mountains their name.*

	Apache Lake	Bartlett Lake	Canyon Lake	Horseshoe Lake	Lake Pleasant	Roosevelt Lake	Saguaro Lake	Verde River (below Horseshoe)	Verde River (below Bartlett)
BOAT RENTAL	●		●		●	●	●		
MOTOR LIMITS									
BOATS ALLOWED	●	●	●	●	●	●	●	●	●
CAMP NEARBY	●	●	●	●	●	●	●	●	●
STORE	●					●	●		
BULLHEAD									
CARP	●	●	●	●	●	●	●	●	●
TILAPIA					●		●	●	
WALLEYE	●		●				●		
NORTHERN PIKE									
CATFISH (Flathead)	●	●		●		●		●	
CATFISH (Channel)	●	●	●	●	●	●	●	●	●
SUNFISH	●	●	●	●	●	●	●	●	●
CRAPPIE	●	●	●	●	●	●	●		
STRIPED BASS					●				
WHITE BASS					●				
SM.MOUTH BASS	●	●	●	●		●	●	●	●
LG.MOUTH BASS	●	●	●	●	●	●	●	●	●
CUTTHROAT									
GRAYLING									
BROOK									
NATIVE									
BROWN									
RAINBOW	●		●				●		●
FLY & LURE ONLY									
ELEVATION	1900	1600	1660	2200	1700	2200	1600	1800	1300
AVERAGE DEPTH (IN FEET)	240	100	130	30	70	110	90		
AVERAGE ACREAGE	2500	2015	926	790	2000	13,000	1100		

REGION 5 FISHING

WHITE MOUNTAIN AREA
REGION 6
CAMPGROUNDS

So many back roads thread through the White Mountains and the forested country of east-central Arizona, an avid explorer could wear out a set of tires before driving them all.

Camp in this region and there's a chance you'll pitch your tent or park your RV where Francisco Vasquez de Coronado and his conquistadors trod way back in 1540. They came up from Mexico looking for the mythical Seven Golden Cities of Cibola. Coronado and his men are considered the first Europeans to have explored this part of Arizona.

Today, U.S. Route 191 has been dubbed "the Coronado Trail." It is not what you'd call a high-speed highway. In some places the road switches back and forth at such sharp angles that driving at more than 15 mph would be excessive. But recreationists don't travel the Coronado Trail for convenience; they travel it for great scenery between the high desert at Clifton and the forested countryside at Alpine and Springville, representing an elevation difference of about 5,000 feet.

Region 6 campgrounds take in parts of the Fort Apache (also called White Mountain Apache) Indian Reservation, which along with the neighboring Apache-Sitgreaves

(OPPOSITE) *Dense alpine forests, lush mountain meadows, and trout-filled lakes and streams make the White Mountains of eastern Arizona a camper's paradise. Here the East Fork of the Black River winds its way toward Three Forks, south of Springerville.*

(ABOVE) *A glimpse into the rugged, remote Blue River country along the Arizona-New Mexico border shows that more than just the river is blue.*

National Forest, is sprinkled with trout lakes and streams set in superlative landscapes. Baldy Peak, at 11,590 feet, is the White Mountain centerpiece, and throughout this region, herds of elk and deer, and flocks of turkeys, are common.

To the east the rugged ranges of Blue River country reach into New Mexico. Wilderness area rules say, "no motorized vehicles," and this may be as close as you can get to experiencing a wilderness without actually resorting to foot or horseback. You can wade the rivers, creeks, and brooks in these parts most of the year; nevertheless they satisfy fishermen.

As if in dramatic counterpoint, as you approach the northern reaches of Region 6, you drop out of the pine-clad White Mountains, through rugged volcanism, and onto the fringes of the Painted Desert. Just off U.S. Route 191 between Springerville and St. Johns, Lyman Lake has been created from the impounded waters of the Little Colorado River. What could be better on an autumn afternoon than to set up your camp in this state park, put your boat in the water, and peacefully watch the sun go down?

On Indian reservations in Arizona, camping rules and regulations differ somewhat from those of the national forests. You cannot camp just anywhere, but must use designated campgrounds. Rarely, if ever, though, will camp space not be available.

① **ALPINE DIVIDE** campground is about four miles north of the high-country community of Alpine, along the east side of U.S. Route 191. It is laid out in a grove of ponderosa pines playfully infiltrated by Abert squirrels. The campground, less than a mile down the road from the 8,453-foot-elevation bench mark is . . . well . . . alpine. If you've been to Yellowstone National Park, you'll see a similarity, but this campground is more than 2,000 feet higher. Just like at Yellowstone,  you're likely to see roving bands of elk, usually in early morning and evening. In late summer and early fall, morning mist hangs on the meadows and honking Canada geese regularly announce that they're rising. A couple of miles north on U.S. 191 is Forest Service Road 56, which takes you to the head of the Escudilla National Recreational Trail and the jump-off point into Escudilla Mountain Wilderness. Is this great camping country or what?!

② **BENNY CREEK** campground, about three miles north of Greer, lies just south of where Benny Creek runs under State Route 373. When full, the campground resembles an RVer's version of "circle the wagons." Although essentially an overflow facility for the award-winning Rolfe C. Hoyer campground, Benny Creek has some enjoyable qualities of its own.

For example, it is just inside a ponderosa patch at the edge of an elk meadow. Also nearby is Rosey Creek. Benny and Rosey were local lovers in the late 1800s. Rosey ran off with Fred, however, leaving Benny heartbroken. The creeks, being apart as they are, supposedly symbolize that Benny and Rosey never got together. But while Benny and Rosey, the lovers, may have remained apart, the two streams become one about three-quarters of a mile before running into the West Fork of the Little Colorado River. Now, for those who love to fish: water from the Little Colorado River creates three nearby reservoirs, Bunch, River, and Tunnel. They are sometimes referred to collectively as "the Greer lakes." All three are well-stocked with rainbow and brown trout.

(OPPOSITE) *Towering ponderosa pines surround Alpine Divide campground. The red bark of these ancient giants smells like vanilla.*
(ABOVE) *Young Rocky Mountain elk graze in a White Mountain horse pasture. When full grown, a bull elk can weigh 1,100 pounds.*

#	RECREATION SITE	APPROX. ELEVATION	SEASONS OF USE	DAYS - LIMIT	FEE	APPROX. NO. OF UNITS	TRAILER LIMIT (FT)	SAFE WATER	RV DUMP STATION	RESTROOMS	SHOWERS	CONTACT INFORMATION
1	Alpine Divide	8500	May Sep.	14	●	12	12	●		●		NFS1A
2	Benny Creek	8250	May Sep.	14	●	26	24	●		●		NFS1A
3	*Big Lake Rec. Area	9100	May Sep.	14	●	205	Call	●	●	●	●	NFS1D
4	Blue Crossing	6200	Apr. Nov.	14		4	16	●		●		NFS1D
5	*Buffalo Crossing	7600	May Oct.	14	●	16	20	●		●		NFS1D
6	Diamond Rock	7900	May Oct.	14	●	12	10	●		●		NFS1A
7	Drift Fence Lake	8000	May Sep.		●	20	Call			●		IR1
8	*Hannagan	9150	May Oct.	14		8	16	●		●		NFS1A
9	Hawley Lake	8500	All Yr.		●	100	Call	●		●		IR1
10	Honeymoon	5600	May Sep.	14		4	16			●		NFS1C
11	Horseshoe Cienega Lake	8500	All Yr.		●	70	Call	●		●		NFS1C
12	*K.P. Cienega	9000	May Sep.	14		5	16	●		●		NFS1C
13	Lower Log Road	6500	May Oct.		●	40	Call			●		IR1
14	▲ Luna Lake	8050	May Sep.	14		53	32	●	●	●		NFS1A
15	*Lyman Lake	6000	All Yr.	15	●	61	Call	●	●	●	●	ASP8
16	Los Burros	7900	May Oct.	14		10	22			●		NFS1E
17	Pacheta Lake	8500	May Sep.		●	25	Call			●		IR1
18	Reservation Lake	9500	May Sep.		●	90	Call	●		●		IR1
19	*Rolfe C. Hoyer	8500	May Sep.	14	●	100	32	●	●	●	●	NFS1D
20	Shush Be Tou Lake	7600	May Oct.		●	20	Call			●		IR1
21	Shush Be Zahze Lake	7500	May Oct.		●	20	Call			●		IR1
22	South Fork	7900	Apr. Nov.	14	●	12	32	●		●		NFS1D
23	Sunrise Lake	9200	All Yr.		●	200	Call	●		●		IR1
24	Upper Blue	6300	May Oct.	14		3	16			●		NFS1C
25	Upper Log Road	6500	May Oct.		●	120	Call			●		IR1
26	West Fork	7600	May Oct.	14		20	10			●		NFS1D
27	Winn	9400	May Oct.	14	●	63	40	●		●		NFS1D

REGION 6 RECREATION SITES

D Dispersed Camping
* Handicapped access
^ Tents only

FACILITIES

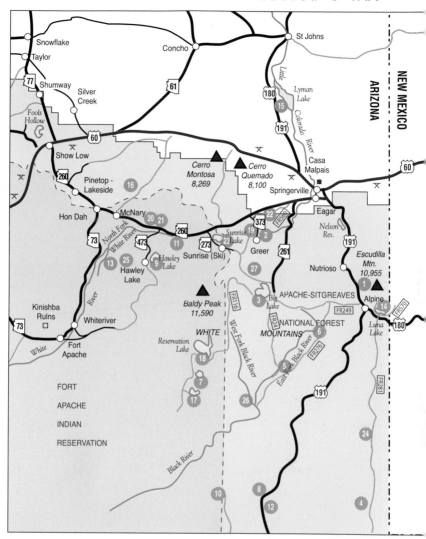

ARIZONA

NEW MEXICO

Snowflake

Taylor

Concho

St Johns

77

Shumway

Silver Creek

61

180

Lyman Lake

15

Colorado River

191

Fools Hollow

60

Show Low

Casa Malpais

60

260

Pinetop - Lakeside

16

Cerro Montosa 8,269

Cerro Quemado 8,100

Springerville

Eagar

Hon Dah

McNary

North Fork White River

20 21

22 373

FR560

Nelson Res.

191

73

473

260

273

11

Sunrise Lake

19

23

2

261

Escudilla Mtn. 10,955

13 25

Hawley Lake

9

Hawley Lake

Sunrise (Ski)

Greer

27

Nutrioso

1

Baldy Peak 11,590

River

Kinishba Ruins

Whiteriver

73

White

Fort Apache

FR116

3

Big Lake

APACHE-SITGREAVES

FR249

NATIONAL FOREST

6

Alpine

14

FR570

FR280

Luna Lake

180

WHITE

MOUNTAINS

FR24

West Fork Black River

East Fork Black River

FR276

Reservation Lake

18

191

FR281

7

17

26

24

FORT

APACHE

INDIAN

RESERVATION

Black River

10

8

12

4

Kingman

Flagstaff

Payson

Phoenix

Yuma

Tucson

■ Dates are approximate. Check with managing agencies if you are planning a trip near the start or end of the season. Contact information is on pages 186-192, where management agencies are listed alphabetically. The first two or three letters in the code for each campground designate the agency. The number and letters following the initial letters designate regions or districts.

▲ Closed for maintenance. Call (928) 339-4384 for reopening information.

127

❸ BIG LAKE campgrounds (there are four) are scattered along the southeast shore of Big Lake, 28 paved miles southwest of Eagar. These White Mountain environs are extravaganzas of natural attractions: 11,590-foot Mount Baldy; high-country meadows; forests of fir, spruce, and aspen; wildlife large and small; hiking and nature trails; and excellent fishing for rainbow, brook, and cutthroat trout. This may sound stereotypical, but it matches the ultimate desires of about 90 percent of the campers. All four of the Apache-Sitgreaves National Forest campgrounds are within easy walking distance of each other and the store, and all have fishy names: Rainbow, Grayling, Cutthroat, and Brookchar. Rainbow, the centerpiece with 150 or so units for tents and RVs, is set up with the most camping conveniences for the urbane outdoor person — paved loops,

widely spaced units, hookups, potable water, deluxe restrooms, showers, and a marina. There is no pavement at the other three campsites, but they have ample conveniences. Grayling perhaps has the most secluded sites for RVs and tents. Cutthroat (about 18 units) and Brookchar (about 12 units) are reserved for tenters. Winter comes early and leaves late at an elevation hovering around 9,100 feet. Despite a short camping season and long distances to major population centers, Big Lake is enormously popular. But don't despaire if you find the sites all filled: There's overflow camping in the open forest not far away. From State Route 260 about 3 miles west of Eagar, take SR 261 south to the Big Lake complex. Or take SR 273 from 260 to the lake.

④ **BLUE CROSSING** campground is in the heart of the Blue Range Primitive Area. The site is small — four units — but big in solitude. Why is it called Blue? Well, as you drive from U.S. 191 down a steep-sided ridge, sunlight, especially in the early morning, gives a pronounced blue cast to the landscape. Scenery along the road into Blue River Crossing is noteworthy, with broken red cliffs reminiscent of Arizona's famous Oak Creek Canyon/Sedona country. People who come to this primitive range generally are self-sufficient campers who want to get away from it all. The campground sits in a dense grove of ponderosas just a couple of hundred feet from the river. From 191 between Hannagan Meadow and Alpine, take Forest Service Road 567 (Red Hill Road) for about 13 miles to Blue Crossing. FR 281 provides an alternate route between Blue

Crossing and U.S. Route 180, about 4 miles east of Alpine. On either road you'll lose or gain, depending upon your direction of travel, about 2,000 feet of elevation. The distance via FR 281 is about 20 miles beyond the pavement, and the road parallels the river much of the way. Prominent as streams go in Arizona, the Blue River is home to fat rainbow and brown trout, but few fisher folk flock to the shallow stream. Wildlife

(OPPOSITE) *Autumn brings spectacular color and exceptional fishing to Big Lake. At more than 9,000 feet elevation, camping here calls for a warm sleeping bag.*
(ABOVE) *The rugged Red Hills stand as a landmark for adventurers en route to remote Blue Crossing campground south of Alpine.*

recognizes this primitive land as a haven and you may see all members of the food chain, from mountain lions on down.

⑤ BUFFALO CROSSING can be reached by several back-country routes. The easiest is to drive about a dozen miles south from Big Lake on FR 24, cross the bridge, hang a left, and there you are. (Reminder: Don't leave home without a Forest Service map.) When driving to Buffalo Crossing you have to try hard not to see any flocks of Merriam's turkeys. The campground stretches along the east side of the East Fork of the Black River in an idyllic setting of ponderosa and riverside willow. Rainbow, brown, brook, and Arizona native trout, and smallmouth bass negotiate the riffles, runs, and back eddies — exemplary fly fishing here. And there's the occasional great blue heron standing in the East Fork doing a little fishing of its own. Buffalo Crossing is a peculiar name for an Arizona place. Except for prehistoric bison, buffalo are not native to the state.

⑥ DIAMOND ROCK campground is about a dozen miles west of Alpine via FRs 249, 276, and 276B. (This latter is essentially a cul-de-sac off FR 276.) The 12-unit campground is situated on the east side of the East Fork of the Black River amid dense conifer forest and thick ground cover. This is not the place to get a sun tan, but it's great for escaping big-city stress. To reach the campground, you must descend into a steep-sloped canyon via a narrow zigzag road. Because of close-knit willows and brush, the stream is difficult to fish. But fishable it is. Rewards include rainbow, brown, brook, and Arizona native trout, and smallmouth bass. Proceeding upstream, the river narrows and becomes shallower. Expect smaller fish, but on light tackle, they're terrific sport.

7 DRIFT FENCE LAKE campground, on the White Mountain Apache Reservation, is set amid aspens and conifers. In morning and evening, the lake often becomes a mirror, reflecting lakeside trees. Its beauty would even enchant Shah Jahan, builder of the Taj Mahal. Being shallow, the lake may lose its fish to winter freezing, but it is generously restocked with rainbow and brook trout in the spring. This

means the biggest fish are caught in late summer and fall. Drift Fence is primitive, so you must be self-contained. There are graded cross-reservation roads that will get you here, but the easiest route starts at Big Lake (No. 3 in this chapter) and passes by Reservation Lake on its way to Drift Fence. The lake is about 3 miles southwest of Reservation Lake on Y20. See Reservation Lake (No. 18 in this chapter) for more directions.

8 HANNAGAN campground is 23 miles south of Alpine via U.S. Route 191, and just off the highway on Forest Service Road 29B. The eight-unit campground in an airy patch of conifers and aspen is easy-in and easy-out for RVers. Bow hunters like to warm their feet at campfires here during season. When I was here, some locals recommended that I drive what they called the "Hannagan Loop." From the campground, head north on U.S. 191 and hang a left onto FR 576 for 4 miles, go right on FR 24 for about 8 miles, then right for another 12 miles on FR 26 back to the pavement. Total estimated camp-to-camp distance is about 32 miles. Drive slow and stay alert for elk, deer, turkey, squirrel, chipmunk, blue grouse, and a good variety of birds. Maybe you'll even see a bear or an eagle.

(OPPOSITE) *While there are no buffalo at Buffalo Crossing, it has everything a traditional camp should offer — forest, lush meadows, and a sparkling stream.* (ABOVE) *Pristine Drift Fence Lake is a seldom-crowded camp in the remote reaches of the Fort Apache Indian Reservation.*

⑨ HAWLEY LAKE campground sits beside the lake of the same name. The lake was created with the impounded waters of Trout Creek and named for Albert M. Hawley, one-time superintendent of the Fort Apache Indian Reservation. Developed in the late 1950s, Hawley Lake was the first reservoir built by the White Mountain Apaches in an endeavor to attract the recreation-minded — and thereby boosting the tribe's economy. Today, Hawley still ranks at the top of the reservation's recreation list. Besides the campground, there are cabins, a marina with rental boats, a general store, a service station, and a trailer-RV park that are available from April to November. Most campgrounds of the White Mountain Apache are in beautiful areas. But this one just happens to hug

the south shore of a 260-acre lake. Fisher folk catch mostly rainbows, but you can also expect to hook an occasional brown, cutthroat, or brook trout. When the lake freezes over, its popularity doesn't stop. On some wintry days there'll be more people fishing through the ice than there are by boat or along the shore during warm weather. From State Route 260 about 11 miles east of Hon Dah, between mileposts 268 and 269, turn south on State Route 473. After 9 miles, the road forks. Bear right, cross the dam, and take any of several dirt roads leading into a forested campsite area. In fall, the aspens put on a spectacular golden display. Even if you decide not to camp here, make the drive.

⑩ HONEYMOON campground, about 24 miles north of Clifton on U.S. Route 191, then 22 miles west and north on FR 217, sits on the banks of Eagle Creek. You'll drop more than a thousand feet from the highway to this hideaway. Even seasoned campers refer to this tiny four-unit site as an out-of-the-way place. The "honeymoon" appellation came about, so the story goes, because Forest Ranger Johnny Wheatly once honeymooned with his bride in a Forest Service cabin nearby. Eagle Creek, which runs into the Gila River about 70 miles south, is one of the network of streams draining the White Mountains. In the early 1880s, a military scouting expedition

saw eagles roosting in the rhyolite bluffs near where the ranger cabin was later built. Doubtless they were the predecessors of the birds that reside in this vicinity today. Also watch for great blue herons, American kestrels, red-tail hawks, mule and white-tail deer, rabbits, coyotes, and chipmunks. Campers who appreciate the work of poets such as Victoria Sackville-West will appreciate Honeymoon:

The country habit has me by the heart,
For he's bewitched forever who has seen,
Not with his eyes but with his vision,
Spring flow down the woods and stippled leaves with sun.

⑪ HORSESHOE CIENEGA LAKE campground sits beside a high-country meadow/marsh rimmed with conifers and aspens. On the entire Fort Apache Indian Reservation, this camp rates second in conveniences only to Hawley Lake. The tribe operates a store here during warm months, where you can buy camping supplies, get permits, and rent boats. The lake (elec-

tric motors only) has a paved boat ramp and a dump station. During winter, the road is kept plowed for those who like ice fishing for rainbows, browns, and brook trout. Like Hawley Lake, Horseshoe Cienega is popular at that time of year, and sometimes fishing contests are held here. It is not uncommon to see several snowmobilers skimming across the landscape, bound to or from the lake, or just enjoying the winterscape. The turnoff to Horseshoe Cienega Lake, created in a horseshoe bend in Bog Creek, is on the south side of S.R. 260 between mileposts 370 and 371 about 11 miles east of its junction with S.R. 73 in Hon Dah. You can see the lake about a mile from the highway. After crossing the dam, bear left to campsites on the lake's south side.

(OPPOSITE) *Hawley Lake is the gem of reservation recreation sites.*
(TOP) *Honeymoon campground lives up to its name — unless you bring the kids.*
(ABOVE) *An iced-over lake doesn't deter these fishermen in the White Mountains.*

⑫ **K.P. CIENEGA** is about 30 miles south of Alpine on U.S. Route 191, then 1.5 miles east on FR 155. The five loosely spaced units of this campground lie on a loop road just inside the fringes of the conifer and aspen forest. Cienega comes from the Spanish word for "marsh," and the creek flows in and out of a tranquil reservoir — adding a halcyon mood to the setting. Small rainbows forage in the runs, riffles, and back eddies. Catching them is great fun on light tackle. Of interest to hikers is nearby access to several trails that penetrate Bear Wallow Wilderness: cross the highway and take FR 25 a few miles to the trailheads. One of the foremost incentives for camping at K.P. Cienega, and other sites along U.S. Route 191, is the opportunity to drive the Coronado Trail (U.S. Route 191). In the 123 miles from Clifton to Springerville, the wide range in elevation sustains an equally wide diversity of flora and fauna.

There are many things to see and do along this sparsely traveled route if you are in the mood to take your time and travel what may be the most twisted two-lane in Arizona. Speed signs sometimes indicate 10 miles per hour. Scenic? Yes! But rare is the knowing motorist who considers U.S. Route 191 a through highway.

⑬ **LOWER LOG ROAD** camping consists of dispersed sites along the North Fork of the White River on the White Mountain reservation. From the traffic circle (see below) you can reach Upper Log Road (No. 25 in this chapter). Take State Route 73 for 4.1 miles south of its junction with 260 at Hon Dah. Turn left (east) at a road marked for Williams Creek Hatchery. Go 0.9 mile, turn right at the T-junction and later bear right at a Y junction that's part of a traffic circle, then quickly bear left. Later, bear left at a fork. Or, from 73 at Milepost 351 north of Whiteriver, turn right (east) on Roberts Ranch Road and follow signs for the Williams hatchery.

(OPPOSITE) *Aspens decorate A-1 Lake along S.R. 260 a few miles east of Horseshoe Cienega Lake. The Army gave Apache Chief Alchesay the name A-1.* (ABOVE) *K.P. Cienega campground lies near trailheads leading into the Bear Wallow Wilderness, some of the wildest country in eastern Arizona.*

⑭ LUNA LAKE campground is three miles east of Alpine off U.S. Route 180, and about a quarter-mile north of Luna Lake on FR 570. Forest engineers fitted it into the open ponderosa pines at the edge of what is known as Bush Valley. It's named not for the vegetation, but for Anderson Bush, who arrived here in 1876. Agricultural experts have called Bush Valley, at nearly 8,000 feet above sea level, the highest place in America where one can successfully grow crops. Luna Lake was created by impounding the headwaters of the San Francisco River. The San Francisco crosses into New Mexico a couple of miles to the east, then meanders around, gaining width and depth, and comes back into Arizona about 40 miles south. If you drove up from southern Arizona on U.S. Route 191, you crossed it at Clifton. Luna Lake is a 200-acre fishing hole stocked with rainbow, cutthroat, and Arizona native trout. In early fall you may have it entirely to yourself. The upper end is a wildlife refuge where nesting cinnamon teal, Canada geese, mallards, and

other waterfowl get priority from April to August. Take your binoculars. You may also see muskrats and the occasional beaver.

⑮ LYMAN LAKE STATE PARK, 18 miles north of Springerville on combined U.S. Route 191/180, sits in a red, tan, and black landscape that could be used for a Star Trek "alien world" location. This is the southernmost end of the Painted Desert and had you been camping here 5 million years ago you'd have been under the waters of vast Lake Bidahochi. Forty-five minutes south rise the White Mountains, extinct volcanoes whose slopes have long since covered themselves with pine and fir. Also, more than 200 cinder cones punctuate this region, and their lava flows stretch onto the high desert for dozens of miles. The elevation here is about 6,000 feet, the camp loops are paved, some include their own ramadas, and there are even showers. And, unlike most places nowadays, Lyman Lake allows beach camping. There are dramatic views

136

from a low hill that overlooks the lake and the main part of the campground. Here's something else that's fun. From Memorial Day to Labor Day, the park people conduct twice-a-day boat tours across the lake so you can see an outstanding collection of prehistoric petroglyphs (drawings scratched on rocks). With a store, marina, and other conveniences, there's rarely any reason to run into town for supplies. The lake, created from waters of the Little Colorado River to provide irrigation for the community of St. Johns, covers 1,500 acres and allows all kinds of water sports. Named for Mormon Bishop Francis M. Lyman, it is a warm-water reservoir and therefor contains largemouth bass, walleye, channel catfish, and crappies. From a recreational point of view, Lyman lake and park are underused. If you would like to have your own 3-mile-long lake some autumn weekend, this is the place.

16 LOS BURROS campground beckons bicycle riders, hikers, and those who just want to relax in a campsite and soak up

area history. A barn and corral, listed in the National Register of Historic Places, remain at what was a forest service ranger station built in the first decade of the 20th century. Los Burros spring still trickles just east of the cabin, but its water is not considered potable. A meadow stretches out from the campground, which is dotted with aspen trees. The relatively flat forest service road leading here and roads venturing from that road into forestland, provide a ideal routes for riders who want to enjoy scenery rather than challenge hills and rocky trails. From State Route 260 in McNary, turn north on the Vernon-McNary Road (also signed Apache County 3140). After 3 miles bear right on Forest Service Road 224 and drive 4 miles to Los Burros in the Apache-Sitgreaves forest.

(OPPOSITE) *Settlers from Luna, New Mexico, moved to the Alpine area and named Luna Lake for their former home town. Luna is Spanish for "moon."* (ABOVE) *Campers at Los Burros have access to relatively flat roads in the White Mountains for easy bicycling. Also, a trailhead is near the campground.*

🄱 PACHETA LAKE dispersed camping area is tough to get to. Your vehicle will take some jolts following the backcountry roads necessary to get to this part of the Apache reservation. You may find Y55 dustier than you like. But if it has rained recently, think mud bog. We're talking low-gear running, so if you're the sort who looks at your watch a lot, you haven't got the time and/or the patience. But for those whose main motivators are tranquillity and trout — both of which are available in abundance — Pacheta Lake is worth it. Facilities at the camping area are down considerably from deluxe, so you must be self-contained. Pacheta Lake is eight miles from Reservation Lake. Head south on Y20, then east on Y55. Good luck. (See Reservation Lake for complete directions.)

🄲 RESERVATION LAKE is another green-spangled paragon well-stocked with rainbows, browns, and brooks. Anglers are prone to look up from their fishing and gaze in fascination at the surrounding stands of conifer and aspen. North and slightly west is the 11,590-foot summit of Baldy Peak. From the camp, which spreads out inside the tree line on both sides of the lake, grassy contours slant to the water's edge. A word of

caution: some loops are so tight that negotiating them while pulling anything bigger than a small tent trailer requires exceptional skill. While this camp is on the Fort Apache Indian Reservation, it is best approached from Big Lake via Forest Routes 249E and 116. After traveling about seven miles west and south on the forest routes you'll cross the national forest/reservation boundary and be on Apache Route Y20. You'll see the lake immediately.

🄳 ROLFE C. HOYER is the campground after which all new campgrounds should be modeled. At least that seems to express the feeling of many who have been here. Located about a mile north of Greer along State Route 373, Hoyer has flush toilets, showers, and other conveniences of home. Combine that with the camp's proximity to the sophisticated little resort town of Greer, and you'll not have to miss out on any creature comforts. Still, Hoyer is set in an open stand of ponderosa pines and the "camping feel" is pervasive. All the sights, sounds, and scents, plus abundant wildlife, can be found in this camp. Fishing is just across the highway in the East and West Forks of the Little Colorado River. Though brook-size, these streams support rainbow, brown, brook, and Arizona native trout. Also nearby

are three impoundments, Tunnel, River, and Bunch Reservoirs. Also, see Benny Creek (No. 2) in this chapter.

⑳ SHUSH BE TOU LAKE (Big Bear Lake) camp units are spaced well apart on largely horizontal ground, making it easy to park large RVs, which have access to a circle drive passing individual sites. This Fort Apache Reservation camp is even accessible in bad weather. During an early September visit I saw more Abert squirrels than outdoor folks, and the sun-dappled spaces among the ponderosa pines were well policed. Fisher folk will find easy access to the lake from the shore or via a paved boat ramp and can expect to have good luck catching rainbow, brown, and brook trout. The lake is formed by a dam on Bog Creek, which comes by the name deservedly. In pioneer days, wagons traveling between Show Low and Springerville did, indeed, bog down when they tried to cross. Getting to either Shush Be Tou or Shush Be Zahze (No. 21 in this chapter)campground is easy. About 11 miles east of Hon Dah on State Route 260, between mileposts 268 and 269, turn north on an unmarked road. After 0.2 mile you'll come to a fork with signs pointing to the lakes. Both campgrounds have portable toilets, picnic tables, and fire rings.

㉑ SHUSH BE ZAHZE LAKE (Little Bear Lake) campground is reached from State Route 260 via the same road as Big Bear Lake (No. 20 above) — turn left at the fork. At 15 acres, Little

---

(OPPOSITE) *Reservation Lake, south of Mount Baldy, the White Mountains' highest peak, lies just within the Fort Apache reservation boundary.*
(ABOVE) *Rolfe C. Hoyer campground near Greer is the state of the art luxury campground near some of the White Mountains' best fishing.*

Bear Lake is just three acres smaller than Big Bear. How does the camp rate? Call it author bias, but Big Bear gets my nod.

㉒ SOUTH FORK, eight miles west of Eagar via State Route 260 and FR 560, is a deep-woods campground. Except for the last quarter-mile, FR 560 is paved all the way, and in late summer it is a sunflower-lined corridor across a strange and mysterious lava field. Volcanic formations give evidence of a former truly hot time. Ponderosa pine, the dominant trees of western North America, can live to be 600 years old, and those at South Fork look as ancient as sequoias. These trees grow best and biggest in Arizona — up to 200 feet high — at elevations between 5,000 and 8,600 feet and in well-drained soils, like volcanic ash. This makes the South Fork area perfect for them. Here the South Fork of the Little Colorado River is even smaller than little. But, amazingly, these tiny high-country streams do produce fish. Expect four species of trout: rainbows, browns, brook, and Arizona native.

㉓ SUNRISE LAKE sits in prairie-like openness, but the campground is sheltered by privacy screens of conifers and aspens so thick the locale seems primordial. I suggest campers be self-contained, but with a general store and service station back at the junction, and the resort restaurant so near, both urban and camp needs are satisfied. The lake is a great trout fishery year-round. (It's one of Arizona's most popular ice-fishing spots.) Rainbows are the primary fish, but you'll catch brook trout as well. With the lake being about a mile  long, a boat is helpful. It is the only reservation lake where you can use outboard motors, but no more than eight horsepower. In winter, this is one of Arizona's premier skiing areas, but you don't have to be a skier to enjoy Sunrise. Why not take a snowcat to the top of Apache Peak? Getting here is easy via paved State Routes 260 and 273 to Sunrise Lake. The campground is a half-mile beyond Sunrise Resort Lodge. Hang a right at the ski-slope junction, then a quick left into the campground.

24 **UPPER BLUE** is 15 miles southeast of Alpine via U.S. Route 180 and Forest Service Road 281. It sits in a grove of junipers in a narrow, conifer-clad canyon (actually 2,000 feet lower than Alpine). Bring your jacket, even in mid-summer, because the sun arrives late in the morning and sets early in the evening. When a campground has no potable water, the controlling agency usually doesn't charge a fee. But at Upper Blue camping is free and there's abundant cold, clear water flowing from a pipe set in a rock. I testify that the water is safe, as I drank a healthy sample. It may even have curative powers. When I bathed my face in it, I noted an immediate outpouring of stress. Upstream about 4 miles, Blue Creek and Dry Blue Creek combine to become Blue River. Where the river and the canyon widen, the vegetation changes to cottonwoods, sycamores, and willows. Sometimes the latter are so thick it makes it difficult to fish. (See Blue Crossing, No. 4 in this chapter.) There are only a few campsites at Upper Blue, but my inspection in late summer showed this pristine place unoccupied. The Forest Service has thoughtfully provided three-sided Adirondack shelters here, perhaps thinking of tent campers who might get caught in the severe weather that can sometimes hammer this remote mountain retreat.

(OPPOSITE) *Wiley Moore shows off his ice fishing catch at Sunrise Lake on the Fort Apache Indian Reservation.*
(ABOVE) *Adirondack shelters welcome campers at the Upper Blue campground on the Blue River southeast of Alpine.*

㉕ UPPER LOG ROAD is a dispersed camping area along the North Fork of the White River for those who are self-contained. There are more campsites than there are tables, which is just one reason to be self-contained. But the conifer-aspen forest and bubbling stream score 8 or 9 on a scale of 10. The North Fork is a good stream for those who like to flyfish. The proper bug, presented in proper fashion, at the proper time, will likely get you a rainbow, with chances of catching secretive browns, brooks, and maybe a cutthroat. Upper Log Road camping area can be reached from State Route 73 (see Lower Log Road, No. 13 in this chapter). Or, it can be reached from State Route 473 (Hawley Lake Road — see No. 9 in this chapter). About 5 miles south of State Route 260, turn west from 473 onto Reservation Route R76 (some maps list 76 as 651 or Slide Creek Road). At 4 miles you'll pass a memorial on the left to a slain officer. Camping begins just west of here. At North Fork the road splits. Cross the river and continue westward on R27, which eventually leads to Lower Log Road sites.

㉖ WEST FORK is about 27 miles west of Alpine via FRs 249, 276, 25, 68, and 68A. (Don't even think about going there without a Forest Service map.) Although there are 20 units at the site, on my inspection I found there weren't nearly that many tables, grills, and fire rings. There was, however, plenty of space to accommodate 20 parties in the overall dispersed camping area. Typical of White Mountain streams, the West Fork of the Black River is pristine, clear, cold water.

Fishing rates very good but everything is catch-and-release, and lure and fly only. Trout have a natural tendency to swim upstream, and those planted in larger streams, like the Black River, eventually spread throughout a healthy watershed system. Here you can expect rainbows, browns, brooks, and Arizona natives. You don't have to go to Alaska to get an Alaska-look — try West Fork campground.

27 **WINN** campground, with its red-cinder loops and young aspen trees, fits the word "distinctive." It even has speed bumps to slow down any lead-foots that might have taken a wrong turn and entered the campground. As for fishing, you can walk from here to the West Fork of the Little Colorado River, or Lee Valley Lake (just across the road from the camp turnoff) which is a prime fishery for Arizona native trout and Arctic grayling (lure and fly only). And just a few miles south on FR 113 are Crescent and Big lakes, both noted for trout. Winn has most of the conveniences a camper could want, including showers.

Still, you're close enough to Greer, a complete resort town, to run in for a gourmet meal if you're tired of camp cooking. But remember, at 9,300 feet Winn is one of Arizona's highest campgrounds. You'll find yourself huffing and puffing until you've had time to get acclimated. Because of a porous volcanic base, Winn is a winner even on rainy days — there's very little mud. Winn is about 12 miles south of Greer, and easily reached via nine miles of FR 87 (which can be accessed near Rolfe C. Hoyer campground), then go left onto FR 43 for a couple miles before taking another left for a mile on FR 554.

(OPPOSITE) *Upper Log campground provides idyllic sites on the banks of the North Fork of the White River on the Fort Apache reservation.* (ABOVE) *Comfort is the name of the game for this all-day angler.*

REGION 6 FISHING

		Ackre Lake	Becker Lake	Big Lake	Black River	Blue River	Bunch Reservoir	Concho Lake	Crescent Lake	Fools Hollow Lake
FACILITIES	BOAT RENTAL			●					●	
	MOTOR LIMITS		elec	8hp			elec	elec	8hp	8hp
	BOATS ALLOWED	●	●	●	●	●	●	●	●	●
	CAMP NEARBY	●		●	●	●	●		●	●
	STORE			●				●	●	
FISH SPECIES	BULLHEAD									
	CARP									
	TILAPIA									
	WALLEYE									●
	NORTHERN PIKE									
	CATFISH (Flathead)									
	CATFISH (Channel)									●
	SUNFISH							●		●
	CRAPPIE									●
	STRIPED BASS									
	WHITE BASS									
	SM.MOUTH BASS				●					●
	LG.MOUTH BASS							●		●
	CUTTHROAT			●						
	GRAYLING	●								
	BROOK			●	●				●	
	NATIVE	●	●		●					
	BROWN				●	●	●			
	RAINBOW		●	●	●	●	●	●	●	●
	FLY & LURE ONLY	●	●							
	ELEVATION	8850	6900	9000	8500	6200	8250	6300	9040	6250
	AVERAGE DEPTH (IN FEET)	10	10	27			10	6	15	23
	AVERAGE ACREAGE	2	85	450			20	60	100	150

ᴰDispersed Camping

Water	Elevation		
K.P. Creek	8900		
Little Colorado River	7000-9000		
Luna Lake	7890	8	75
Lyman Lake	5980	22	1400
Rainbow Lake	6700	6	80
Reservation Creek	7100		
River Reservoir	8220	20	50
Scotts Reservoir	6720	10	80
Show Low Lake	6540	20	100
Silver Creek	6100		
Tunnel Reservoir	8260	10	15

SOUTHERN ARIZONA
REGION 7
CAMPGROUNDS

C ampers interested in Spanish history and the flavor of Mexico will find Region 7 a fascinating area to explore. One early explorer, Father Eusebio Francisco Kino, established a string of missions, starting in Mexico and penetrating into Arizona as far north as Tucson. Two of these missions, Tumacácori and San Xavier, still stand. The former is protected as a National Historic Park, and the latter continues to minister to the Tohono O'odham Indians.

This is another region that offers something for every camper, from desert lovers to those who think they're not camping unless they are in mountains and conifer forests. Catalina State Park Campground, for example, sits amid desert grasslands at an elevation of 2,700 feet at the base of the Santa Catalina Mountains. Spencer Canyon campground, meanwhile, is at the 8,000-foot level on the mountains proper. (The Santa Catalinas top out at 9,157-foot Mount Lemmon.)

Butting against Tucson's eastern and western city limits are the two units of Saguaro National Park. And near Saguaro National Park West is the world-famous Arizona-Sonora Desert Museum. The last word of the name is misleading.

(OPPOSITE) *The Santa Catalina Mountains tower over Catalina State Park north of Tucson. The 5,500-acre high-desert park and adjoining Coronado National Forest land offer hiking and equestrian trails and abundant bird-watching — more than 150 species call the area home.*

(ABOVE) *South of Tucson the Santa Rita Mountains rise to more than 9,000 feet elevation. Hikers, campers, and bird-watchers flock to Madera Canyon on the western flank of the range.*

This is no dank place of flower pictures and stuffed animals, but a botanical garden and zoo where flora and fauna live and thrive in natural settings.

South of Tucson is a second "sky island," as high mountains rising from the desert are called. The Santa Ritas rise abruptly to 9,453 feet above sea level at Mount Wrightson. Within their folds lies Madera Canyon, about which every serious bird-watcher knows. More than 200 species have been seen here, with emphasis on the elegant (coppery-tailed) trogon. The camp areas in this book usually have hiking trails nearby, and the Santa Ritas have more than 70 miles of them.

In the southeast corner of the region is still another sky island, the Huachuca Mountains, where Miller Peak reaches 9,466 feet above sea level. At the base of its eastern slope, off State Route 92, is Ramsey Canyon, which birders know even better than Madera Canyon. The stars of this canyon include 14 species of hummingbirds. The Nature Conservancy, which now owns the canyon, strictly limits visitation, so be sure and call well ahead of your planned trip.

1 BOG SPRINGS campground clings to the west side of the Santa Rita Mountains among the juniper, oaks, and sycamores

of Coronado National Forest. In August, century plants and yuccas, and barrel and prickly pear cacti are in full bloom and/or fruited. The campground loops are paved, but steep and twisting in accordance with the near-vertical topography of the Santa Ritas. You can get a crick in your neck staring up at the peaks in this range. Numerous trails take off from here up toward Mount Wrightson Wilderness. Wrightson tops the range at 9,453 feet, with Mount Hopkins next highest at 8,585 feet. Near the campground entrance, trees shade several picnic areas, and serene Madera Creek tumbles down the canyon. Madera Canyon is especially popular with birdwatchers. If you're going to stay a few days you might want to bring a hummingbird feeder with you. To get here, leave Interstate 19 at Continental (Exit 63) and head east on Forest Service Road 70. The road winds through pecan groves, across grasslands sprinkled with mesquite, and up into the forest for 13 miles. It dead-ends in Madera Canyon, but Bog Springs isn't quite that far.

② CATALINA STATE PARK, just off State Route 77 north of Tucson, sits on high-desert grassland at an elevation of about 2,700 feet. Saguaro, prickly pear, and cholla cacti dot the slopes of the nearby Santa Catalina Mountains, and camp units are pleasantly arranged amid groves of mesquite trees. The park has everything a modern camper might want, including showers. This is one of the best bases in Arizona for seeing a variety of attractions. Swing south around the mountain and across northern Tucson to enjoy the streamside beauty of Sabino Canyon. If you have enough time, continue 30 miles up the Catalina Highway to conifer-forested Mount Lemmon,

9,157 feet above sea level. Heading the other direction from the campground, 10 miles north you can turn onto State Route 79, Pinal Pioneer Parkway. Take a picnic lunch, plan a leisurely trip for the next 30 miles, and from late March through mid-May expect to see great wildflowers and colorful cacti. Or for something completely different, instead of turning onto State Route 79, continue ahead on State Route 77 about five miles to Biosphere 2, a futuristic space frame sheltering seven ecosystems, including a huge self-sustaining ocean. Part of Columbia University's Earth Institute, the complex's demonstration labs are open to visitors. Other suggestions for active campers in the Tucson area are discussed in the Gilbert Ray campground section.

(OPPOSITE) *Southern Arizona attracts hummingbirds like nowhere else. Fourteen species appear in the region throughout the year.*
(ABOVE) *Prickly pear cacti bear fruit in late summer along the road to Catalina State Park. The fruit is tasty, but watch out for the hair-like spines in the skin.*

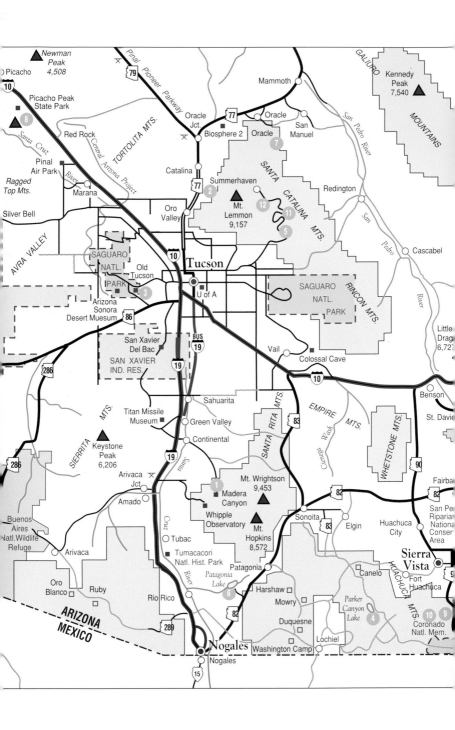

Newman
Peak
4,508

Picacho

Picacho Peak
State Park

Red Rock

Pinal
Air Park

Ragged
Top Mts.

Silver Bell

AVRA VALLEY

SAGUARO
NATL.

PARK

Arizona
Sonora
Desert Muesum

San Xavier
Del Bac

SAN XAVIER
IND. RES.

SIERRITA
MTS.

Keystone
Peak
6,206

Arivaca
Jct

Amado

Buenos
Aires
Natl.Wildlife
Refuge

Arivaca

Oro
Blanco

Ruby

ARIZONA
MEXICO

Pinal
Pioneer Parkway

Oracle
Jct.

Biosphere 2

Catalina

Oro
Valley

Old
Tucson

Central Arizona Project

TORTOLITA MTS.

Santa Cruz

River

Marana

Mammoth

Oracle

Oracle

Summerhaven

Mt.
Lemmon
9,157

Tucson

U of A

SANTA CATALINA MTS.

San
Manuel

Redington

Kennedy
Peak
7,540

GALIURO

MOUNTAINS

San Pedro River

San

Pedro

River

Cascabel

SAGUARO
NATL.

PARK

RINCON MTS.

Little
Drag
6,72

Vail

Colossal Cave

Titan Missile
Museum

Sahuarita

Green Valley

Continental

Madera
Canyon

Whipple
Observatory

Tubac

Tumacacori
Natl. Hist. Park

Patagonia

Patagonia
Lake

Rio Rico

Harshaw

Mowry

SANTA RITA MTS.

Mt. Wrightson
9,453

Mt.
Hopkins
8,572

Sonoita

EMPIRE   MTS.

Cienega   Wash

Benson

St. David

WHETSTONE MTS.

Elgin

Huachuca
City

Canelo

Parker
Canyon
Lake

Fairba

San Pe
Riparia
Nationa
Conser
Area

Sierra
Vista

Fort
Huachuca

HUACHUCA

Duquesne

Lochiel

Coronado
Natl. Mem.

MTS.

Washington Camp

Nogales

Nogales

Santa   Cruz   River

REGION 7 RECREATION SITES *Handicapped access ^ Tents only	APPROX. ELEVATION	SEASONS OF USE ■	DAYS - LIMIT	FEE	APPROX. NO. OF UNITS	TRAILER LIMIT (FT)	FACILITIES				CONTACT INFORMATION ■
							SAFE WATER	RV DUMP STATION	RESTROOMS	SHOWERS	
① Bog Springs	5200	All Yr.	14	●	13	22	●		●		NFS3B
② *Catalina State Park	2750	All Yr.	15	●	120	Call	●	●	●	●	ASP3
③ *Gilbert Ray	2600	All Yr.	7	●	160	Call	●	●	●		CRP3A
④ Lakeview	5400	All Yr.	14	●	65	32	●		●		NFS3E
⑤ Molino Basin	4500	Oct. Apr.	14	●	40	22			●		NFS3D
⑥ *Patagonia Lake	4050	All Yr.	15	●	115	Call	●	●	●	●	ASP9
⑦ Peppersauce	4700	All Yr.	14	●	17	22	●		●		NFS3D
⑧ *Picacho Peak	2000	All Yr.	15	●	95	Call	●	●	●	●	ASP10
⑨ Ramsey Vista	7400	All Yr.	14	●	8	12			●		NFS3E
⑩ Reef Townsite	7200	All Yr.	14	●	14	16	●		●		NFS3E
⑪ *Rose Canyon	7200	Apr. Oct.	14	●	74	22	●		●		NFS3D
⑫ *Spencer Canyon	8000	Apr. Oct.	14	●	62	22	●		●		NFS3D

■ Kingman   ■ Flagstaff

■ Payson

■ Phoenix

■ Yuma

■ Tucson

③ GILBERT RAY campground lies west of Tucson, over the mountains and through the saguaros, via Speedway Boulevard and Gates Pass. It is part of the Pima County Parks system and you can expect all the amenities. Gilbert Ray is extremely popular with winter sun-chasers, hence the "Campground Full" sign is posted with regularity. The camp sits in a spectacular part of the Sonoran Desert, and just three miles northwest on Kinney Road is the Arizona-Sonora Desert Museum. The term "museum" is misleading. No other place

■ Dates are approximate. Check with managing agencies if you are planning a trip near the start or end of the season. Contact information is on pages 186-192, where management agencies are listed alphabetically. The first two or three letters in the code for each campground designate the agency. The number and letters following the initial letters designate regions or districts.

shows off the living flora and fauna of the desert so well. Visitors come from around the world. Continue another few miles west to the western section of Saguaro National Park. This may be the best stand of saguaro cacti on the planet. But if you're looking for livelier entertainment, Old Tucson Studios, a theme park and movie studio/sound stage where hundreds of movies have been filmed, is literally within view of the campground. If you're into history, Mission San Xavier del Bac is only a dozen or so miles away (southeast on Kinney Road and State Route 86, then south on Mission Road). Despite the increased human activity at Gilbert Ray, wildlife is in abundance. You'll see Gambel's quail, cactus wrens, and

numerous other birds fluttering among the thorny vegetation. And in early morning or near dusk, coyotes sometimes trot down loop roads while desert mule deer browse not far off. Other suggestions for active Tucson-area campers are discussed in the Catalina State Park section.

④ LAKEVIEW campground sits in the high-desert grasslands of the rolling Canelo Hills with a backdrop of the hulking Huachuca Mountains to the northeast. Around Parker Canyon Lake, cottonwoods, willows, and marsh grass give the illusion that you're not in Arizona. There's a lakeside store and marina, and you can expect to catch rainbow trout, largemouth bass, sunfish, bullhead, and channel catfish. Historically, William Parker was a "volunteer" from Tennessee. He got lost en route to the California gold fields and wandered into the canyon that would later bear his name. He did well in California, got married, and moved his family to Phoenix. Then in 1881, they came back to this canyon — to escape the "congestion." The most scenic route to Lakeview is from the east via FR 61 through Montezuma Pass (6,575-foot elevation)

(OPPOSITE) *A rainbow signals a pot of gold along the road to Parker Canyon Lake east of the Huachuca Mountains.*
(ABOVE) *Legions of saguaro cacti march over a ridge at Saguaro National Park. Of the park's two units, only the western one has a campground nearby.*

at Coronado National Memorial. The most convenient route, however, heads south from State Route 82 on all-weather but unpaved State Route 83. In about 30 miles you'll be at Parker Canyon Lake and the campground.

⑤ MOLINO BASIN campground, about 6 miles up the Catalina Highway (also called the Mount Lemmon Highway) from Tucson, nests in a deep "V" between two ridges in the Santa Catalina Mountains. Even though the elevation is about

4,500 feet, the environment here is still desert. Although nearly 2,000 feet higher than Catalina State Park, which is on the northern slope of this same mountain, this camp's southern exposure causes it to be several degrees warmer, and therefore Molino closes during summer months. But in contrast, this unusual micro-climate makes for great winter camping at an elevation that normally would be uncomfortably cold. A few saguaros, which generally don't grow above 3,500 feet, can still be seen in this area. Geologically speaking, Molino Basin is made up of metamorphosed granite (Catalina gneiss, pronounced "nice"), and the sandy washes are rich in silvery mica flakes and tiny burgundy "sand rubies" (garnets). That'll give the kids something to look for. At Windy Point, up the road a few miles, spectacular gneiss formations are popular with rock climbers.

⑥ PATAGONIA LAKE STATE PARK lies in rolling hill country about halfway between the communities of Nogales and Patagonia. The campground is laid out exceptionally well amid mesquite trees on the gentle slopes above 260-acre Patagonia Lake. This is a fun place, complete with a sandy beach and all the modern water-recreation conveniences, including a store and marina with rental boats. It is one of Arizona's few "campground lakes" where you can water-ski (during week-days only). A high, single-arch pedestrian bridge spans an arm of

the lake, providing a short-cut for itinerant shore fisher folk and a scenic viewpoint for the rest of us. Although rainbow trout are stocked in Patagonia Lake, it's essentially a warm-water fishery and you're more likely to catch largemouth bass, sunfish, crappies, and channel and flathead catfish. About five miles east is the Patagonia-Sonoita Creek Preserve, a 312-acre wildlife sanctuary of the Nature Conservancy. (It is open to the public.) Coues deer, javelina, and the elusive coatimundi, are among the mammals that call the refuge home. But mainly visitors come to see the more than 200 species of birds that flock here.

(OPPOSITE) *The granitic spires at Standing Rocks keep watch over the Mount Lemmon Highway in the Santa Catalina Mountains.* (ABOVE) *A boy learns the art of fishing at Patagonia Lake State Park, a 250-acre impoundment northeast of Nogales.*

⑦ **PEPPERSAUCE** campground, on your first visit, will come as a surprise. It is situated in the northeastern foothills of the Santa Catalina Mountains. To get here, start at Oracle and head east-southeast on the Mount Lemmon Road. After the pavement ends you will pass through dry desert spiked with ocotillo, cholla, and barrel cacti for about five miles. Suddenly you will top out on a hill and there, a few hundred yards below, a grove of giant sycamores shades the oasis of Peppersauce campground. In summer Peppersauce is a cool retreat from the

desert heat that encircles it. Peppersauce Springs, a short distance up the arroyo, nourish the ancient roots of this giant green canopy. Yes, this is a very popular camp. The name comes from Louie Depew, who, so the story goes, was hooked on pepper sauce (hot sauce) and lamented losing a bottle of it in the wash.

⑧ **PICACHO PEAK STATE PARK** is located on the slopes of the rocky pinnacle by the same name, 35 miles northwest of Tucson along Interstate 10. Picacho, in Spanish, means peak. "Peak peak" may be redundant, but its "sky-touching" visage can be seen from a great distance. In mid-March of some years, desert wildflowers bloom in such profusion as to cause traffic to stop on the interstate. Sometimes there are acres and acres of golden poppies, purple owl clover, and the brilliant magenta of strawberry hedgehog cacti. A scenic drive connects the campground to other areas of pristine desert flora within the park.

The camp is far enough away from the interstate that the noise is not intrusive. There are several challenging hiking trails, and many first-class conveniences, including showers, nearby restaurants, a convenience store, and a gas station. Of historical interest: on April 15, 1862, about a dozen Union soldiers and 16 Confederates fought the westernmost battle of the Civil War near here.

(OPPOSITE, TOP) *Peppersauce campground hides in a sycamore-shaded pocket in the high desert on the north side of the Santa Catalina Mountains.*
(OPPOSITE, BOTTOM) *The Picacho Peak trail winds through spring gold poppies.*
(ABOVE) *In its twisting 26 miles the Mount Lemmon Highway climbs more than 6,000 feet in elevation, taking travelers from cacti to pines in about an hour.*

9 Ramsey Vista and **10 Reef Townsite** campgrounds take some getting-to and only passengers will have time to enjoy the spectacular panoramas along the way. But not to worry — optimism will be rewarded. This general area is the northern extreme of the Chihuahuan Desert. En route to camp you pass from grasslands, through scrub oak and juniper, and at the campground there are conifers. Ramsey Vista, 200 feet higher than Reef Townsite, has an airiness about it and great views just a few feet away. Reef screens you from the sun with its denser forest of mostly ponderosa. At either campground

you feel like you're on top of the world, but Miller Peak, the highest in the Huachuca range, goes on to 9,466 feet. The town of Reef, now vanished, was a mining camp named for the reefs of ore-bearing rock. Frank Ramsey worked cattle in these parts at the turn of the century. He must have been a pretty likable guy to have a peak, canyon, stream, and campground named for him. To get to these campgrounds, go south of Sierra Vista seven miles on State Route 92. Turn right (west) on Carr Canyon Road. The camps are 10 and 11 miles, respectively, on FR 368 up the eastern face of the mountain to an elevation of 7,400 feet. It's a good unpaved road, but narrow, steep, and winding. Watch the skies on your drive up. You may see a golden eagle riding a thermal.

11 Rose Canyon campground grows on you, so to speak. Set in the cool-to-crisp ponderosa-pine country of Coronado National Forest, it's just 16 miles up the Catalina Highway from Tucson's eastern city limits. Because of its proximity to this major metropolitan area, it is especially popular on weekends with locals seeking refuge from desert heat. The forest is open here, there is little underbrush, and paved loops wind

---

(OPPOSITE) *Campers enjoy the fall colors in the Santa Catalina Mountains. At over 9,000 feet elelvation, this sky island range experiences all four seasons.*
(ABOVE) *The road to Reef Townsite and Ramsey Vista campgrounds snakes up the side of the Huachuca Mountains near the Arizona-Mexico border.*

through a number of campground sections to terminate at the Rose Canyon Lake parking lot. It's only about a block from the camp to the lake where rainbow trout and sunfish fin about. The Catalina Highway is popular with bicyclists who get a lift to the top, then coast down 20-some miles to the desert floor. About a mile up the road from the Rose Canyon turnoff is San Pedro Vista, with its spectacular panorama of

Pima and Cochise counties to the east. Nearby Rose Peak rises to 7,299 feet. Three schools of thought compete for the naming: that it was for 1915 miner, L.J. Rose; for the abundance of wild roses found in the area; or for the color of the iron-stained porphyry rock.

⑫ **SPENCER CANYON**, near the top of Mount Lemmon, is a 62-unit campground of the split-level variety. The four areas, called Ponderosa, Eastfork, Turkey Track, and Spencer, are connected by unpaved access roads. The elevation is about 8,000 feet and the park-like pine forest is relatively free of underbrush. For most of us lowlanders, the high elevation makes hiking difficult. Solution: Drive a little farther up the Catalina Highway to the ski lift and enjoy a ride to the top. In fall, when the quaking aspens have flamed from green to yellow, the area makes for an especially rewarding camp trip. You may be surprised to find a "brau haus" near the lift. Getting to Spencer Canyon is easy, it's about 22 uphill miles from Tucson via the Catalina Highway.

(ABOVE) *Rose Canyon Lake offers trout fishing high in the Catalina Mountains.*

		Parker Canyon Lake	Patagonia Lake	Rose Canyon Lake
FACILITIES	BOAT RENTAL	●	●	
	MOTOR LIMITS	8hp		
	BOATS ALLOWED	●	●	
	CAMP NEARBY	●	●	●
	STORE	●	●	
FISH SPECIES	BULLHEAD	●	●	
	WALLEYE			
	NORTHERN PIKE			
	CATFISH (Flathead)		●	
	CATFISH (Channel)	●	●	
	SUNFISH	●	●	●
	CRAPPIE		●	
	STRIPED BASS			
	WHITE BASS			
	SM.MOUTH BASS			
	LG.MOUTH BASS	●	●	
	CUTTHROAT			
	GRAYLING			
	BROOK			
	NATIVE			
	BROWN			●
	RAINBOW	●	●	●
	FLY & LURE ONLY			
	ELEVATION	5400	4050	7000
	AVERAGE DEPTH (IN FEET)	82	90	44
	AVERAGE ACREAGE	125	260	7

REGION 7 FISHING

SOUTHEASTERN ARIZONA
REGION 8
CAMPGROUNDS

T he southeasternmost corner of Arizona, like several other regions described in this book, provides a great variety of elevations and things to see and do in and around this area's "sky islands." These green, pine-covered mountain ranges such as the Chiricahuas, Dragoons, Galiuros, and, highest of all, the Pinalenos, rise abruptly from the surrounding sea of desert.

The Chiricahuas were once a stronghold of Apache Indians. Now there are more bird-watchers and campers than Indians. The birders base themselves at the tiny community of Portal, on the eastern slope, where the lushness of Cave Creek attracts more than 170 species of flying wildlife.

Historically, Portal and nearby Paradise were hangouts for outlaws like the losing participants in the Earp-Clanton O.K. Corral gunfight. In nearby Rustler's Park, where these outlaws temporarily held stolen cattle, campers tread the same ground as Johnny Ringo, Curly Bill Brocius, and the Clanton clan.

Tombstone, at the southwestern edge of this region, lies about 56 straight-line miles from Portal. Add in the zigzagging to get around topographical obstacles and you have to respect both the good guys and bad guys for their seemingly casual

(OPPOSITE) *Nestled into Cave Creek Canyon on the eastern flank of the Chiricahua Mountains, Sunny Flat campground lives up to its name. Beautiful Cave Creek Canyon hosts an impressive variety of plant and animal species and is referred to by many as a miniature Yosemite.*

(ABOVE) *A visitor admires the view of Chiricahua National Monument from Massai Point. Hiking trails wind throughout the erosion-sculptured volcanic rock formations of this otherworldly landscape.*

167

horseback crossings of this rugged region. Still, the historical drama is equaled by the scenic juxtaposition of wide desert grasslands and towering mountain ranges.

1 **ARCADIA**, anchored about halfway up Mount Graham alongside State Route 366 (Swift Trail), is a "split-level" campground. It is situated at an elevation of 6,700 feet, where the transition variety of forest trees includes manzanita, oak, and ponderosa pines. The units have been arranged to conform with the uneven topography and, conveniently, Arcadia National Recreation Trail takes off from this campground. The Mount Graham red squirrel, a threatened species, lives nearby, and the tassel-eared Abert squirrel can also be seen scampering across the forest floor and through the tree tops. The appellation "Arcadia" comes from ancient Greece where it was a region of simple pleasure and quiet — and the name fits! If you happen to find the lower campground full, Arcadia (upper) is just a curtain of trees away.

2 **BONITA CANYON** is pocketed in the 17-square-mile Chiricahua National Monument on the western reaches of the Chiricahua Mountains. It is easily reached about 30 miles south of Interstate 10 via State Route 186. Camping units have been invitingly laid out among low trees, mostly oak and manzanita. The Chiricahua Mountains themselves are rooted in an arid grassland spiked with agave, yucca, and numerous species of cacti. Wildlife is abundant and especially includes white-tailed deer and perhaps a rare thick-billed parrot. Yes, native parrots once flew wild in the United States, and conservation agencies are presently try-ing to re-establish them. Twenty-five million years ago a violent volcanic eruption here produced the stony material geologists call rhyolite, which has eroded into this bizarre, corrugated landscape of lichen-painted monoliths, and balanced and buttressed rocks. The monument's nickname, "The

Wonderland of Rocks," fits perfectly. Excellent hiking trails offer new perspectives every few feet. Anyone who camps here will find an abundance of fascinating views. (Note: several camp units can accommodate trailers up to 22 feet in length.)

CAMP RUCKER (NO. 13), see Rucker Canyon, Page 179.

CAVE CREEK RECREATIONAL AREA has a feeling of power and majesty not unlike Yosemite park (in a scaled-down version). Within a few short miles the canyon contains three highly desirable campgrounds. A bridge now spans the creek that vehicles once had to ford to reach the campgrounds. ③ IDLEWILDE and ④ STEWART are tucked against the southeast wall of the canyon in riparian habitat. ⑤ SUNNY FLAT, meanwhile, spreads across a grassy meadow

on the opposite side. Upon entering Sunny Flat, you'll see the impressive prominent pinnacle called Cathedral Rock rising hundreds of feet above the camp. Each of these camps is only minutes away from the Portal General Store where, among other things, extensive birder supplies are available. Scientists at the Southwest Research Station, just up the canyon a few

(OPPOSITE) *Located in the transition zone between desert and forest, Bonita campground at Chiricahua Naional Monument is filled with yucca and oak.*
(ABOVE) *Cave Creek in the southeastern Chiricahua Mountains flows through a conifer-and-hardwood-filled canyon whose walls are pocked by shallow caves.*

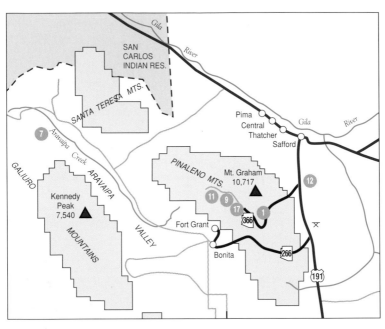

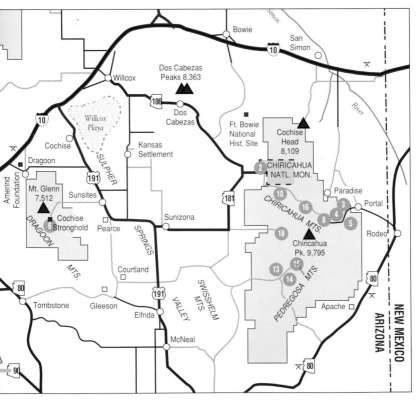

REGION 8 RECREATION SITES *Handicapped access ^ Tents only	APPROX. ELEVATION	SEASONS OF USE	DAYS - LIMIT	FEE	APPROX. NO. OF UNITS	TRAILER LIMIT (FT)	SAFE WATER	RV DUMP STATION	RESTROOMS	SHOWERS	CONTACT INFORMATION
1 Arcadia	6700	All Yr.	14	●	19	22	●		●		NFS3C
2 *Bonita Canyon	5400	All Yr.	14	●	22	29	●		●		NPS2
3 Idlewilde	5000	Apr. Oct.	14	●	10	16	●		●		NFS3A
4 Stewart	5100	All Yr.	14	●	6	22	●		●		NFS3A
5 Sunny Flat	5200	All Yr.	14	●	14	22	●		●		NFS3A
6 *Cochise Stronghold	5000	All Yr.	14	●	10	22	●		●		NFS3A
7 Fourmile Canyon	3500	All Yr.	14	●	10	30	●		●		BLM4
8 ^Herb Martyr	5800	All Yr.	14		7				●		NFS3A
9 ^Hospital Flat	9000	May Nov.	14	●	11				●		NFS3C
10 Pinery Canyon	7000	Apr. Nov.	14		4	16			●		NFS3A
11 *Riggs Flat	8600	May Nov.	14	●	26	22			●		NFS3C
12 *Roper Lake State Pk.	3300	All Yr.	14	●	75	45	●	●	●	●	ASP11
13 Camp Rucker	5600	All Yr.	14	●	12		●		●		NFS3A
14 Cypress Park	6000	Mar. Oct.	14	●	7	16			●		NFS3A
15 Rucker Forest Camp	6500	All Yr.	14	●	14	16	●		●		NFS3A
16 *Rustler Park	8500	Apr. Nov.	14	●	25	22	●		●		NFS3A
17 Shannon	9100	May Nov.	14	●	11	16	●		●		NFS3C
18 Sycamore	6200	Mar. Nov.	14		5	16	●		●		NFS3A

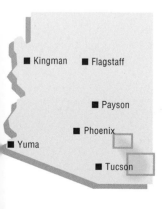

- Kingman
- Flagstaff
- Payson
- Phoenix
- Yuma
- Tucson

■ Dates are approximate. Check with managing agencies if you are planning a trip near the start or end of the season. Contact information is on pages 186-192, where management agencies are listed alphabetically. The first two or three letters in the code for each campground designate the agency. The number and letters following the initial letters designate regions or districts.

miles, say that climatic influences here have created the richest diversity of wildlife in the United States, especially for birds. Visitors come from around the world to study here. Getting to these campgrounds is easy. They're on the five-mile paved portion of Forest Route 42 just west of Portal.

⑥ COCHISE STRONGHOLD is hidden away on the eastern slopes of the Dragoon Mountains. The campground loops are paved and units are carefully laid out amid a jumble of giant boulders and trees. Overall it has a somewhat park-like look. Cochise, the famed Apache chief, and his warriors did in fact

use this area as their stronghold before the peace treaty of 1872. In the period 1861-71, the story goes, Cochise warred on the whites after being attacked under a flag of truce. Cochise's unmarked grave is supposedly in the vicinity of the campground. The exact site was purposely obscured by his warriors, who galloped their horses over it and the entire stronghold area after burying him. To get here, head south of Interstate 10 on U.S. Route 191 to Sunsites (about 12 miles), and about eight miles west on unpaved FR 84 (Ironwood Road).

CYPRESS PARK (NO. 14), see Rucker Canyon, Page 179.

⑦ FOURMILE CANYON is a quarter-mile south of Klondyke on FR 695. It's not hard to get here. Go 12 miles northwest of Safford on U.S. Route 70, then 35 unpaved miles southwest on Klondyke Road. The campground is situated at 3,500 feet in a mesquite flat between the Galiuro and Santa Teresa mountains. Encroaching flora of the high-desert grasslands gives the camp an appearance of being abandoned. Yet this out-of-the-way Bureau of Land Management site has electrically lighted restrooms with wash basins and flush toilets. If you're looking

(OPPOSITE) *The scenic drive to Chiricahua National Monument's Massai Point passes rock formations weighing hundreds of tons perched on narrow pinnacles.* (ABOVE) *Cochise Stronghold campground in the Dragoon Mountains has a manicured, rock garden ambiance.*

for company, Fourmile is not the place to find it. You may have the camp entirely to yourself, even though another nine miles brings you to the entrance of popular Aravaipa Canyon Wilderness. (Fourmile occasionally acts as a base camp for hikers who have permits to enter that restricted area.) At Klondyke there's a Bureau of Land Management branch office, a general store, and little else. Numerous trails head out of this area and into the Santa Teresa and Galiuro mountains. In this "land less traveled" you can, and should, have high expectations of seeing wildlife. Klondyke (spelled with an "i" in Canada) was named by prospectors returning from the Yukon around the turn of the century.

⑧ **HERB MARTYR** campground is tucked into a gulch on the bank of Cave Creek in the Chiricahua Mountains. At the entrance to the campground a masonry dam impounds a skip-stone pool from which the stream playfully cascades down the sloping rockwork. The steep nature of the terrain dictates that the sites be close together, and thus suitable only for tents or small RVs. Still, the attractiveness of this remote camp makes it very popular. Getting here is easy. Head west from Portal, and Herb Martyr is at the end of paved FR 42A just beyond the Southwestern Research Station.

⑨ **HOSPITAL FLAT** campground, 22 steep, twisting miles up State Route 366 (Swift Trail) from U.S. Route 191, sits beside an open, summer-flowered meadow at about 9,000 feet. This is a tent-only campground and you must carry your gear a short distance back into the woods where the sweet smell of conifers fills the air. As you may already have surmised, there is no hospital here. But during the Indian Wars of the 1870s the Army stationed soldiers far below at Fort Grant. During those years this mountain meadow was the site of a cool summer hospital where the wounded and sick were brought to recuperate. Also, officers and their families occasionally spent a few days of cool R&R up here to escape the heat of base housing at Fort Grant.

IDLEWILDE (NO. 3), see Cave Creek Area, Page 169.

⑩ PINERY CANYON campground, at about 7,000 feet, is a semi-flat place smack in the middle of Coronado National Forest. This shady and serene canyon is best suited for small RVs and tents. In fact, those in the know do not even take large RVs on this road because in places it's extremely rocky and washboardy with steep, tight switchbacks. Despite its

remoteness, the camp fills early on warm summer weekends, especially three-dayers like Memorial Day and Labor Day. The Chiricahua Mountains are bear country. While most bears are intimidated by people and machinery and will head away on their own, signs along the road remind you to stay alert. Problems usually come at night because careless campers leave food out, or worse, eat cookies in their sleeping bags. The appetizing smell drifts off on the cool night air and that will bring trouble. The first campers here, and the source of the name, came during frontier times. In the 1860s, the military cut timber in this canyon for the construction of Fort Bowie, about 17 miles north as the crow flies. To get here from the east: start at Portal and go west on FR 42 about 15 miles (the first five are paved). From the west: start at the Chiricahua National Monument entrance and head south and east on FR 42 about the same distance.

⑪ RIGGS FLAT is a pristine place reaching more than a mile and a half toward the stratosphere. What gives this camp-ground the edge over others on the mountain is 11-acre Riggs Flat Lake. At times the lake appears mirror-smooth and reflects the incredible blue of the sky. Humans are instinctive-ly drawn to water, and although the lake contains rainbow and brown trout, fishing may not enter into the decision to camp

(OPPOSITE) *Hikers stroll along the road below towering, eroded volcanic cliff faces near Herb Martyr campground.*
(ABOVE) *Black bears are among the variety of animals that call the Chiricahua Mountains home. Visitors should heed information on how to camp in bear country.*

here. You may just want to look and, as Zen Buddhists say, "empty your mind." Paved loops weave among the conifers which frame the lake under long-needled limbs. Roadside signs warn of bears, which many a camper wants to see and few do. There's a pretty good chance of seeing other wildlife, however, like white-tailed deer. At an elevation of 8,600 feet, Riggs Flat is about 20 degrees cooler than the town of Safford at the mountain's base. On the map these are the Pinaleno

Mountains (Spanish corruption of the Apache word for deer), but locally they are referred to by the name of the highest peak, 10,717-foot-high Mount Graham. The mountain is laced with hiking trails, including one that leads to the top. Most of the trails are steep and demanding, and you need to keep the elevation in mind when you decide to go for a hike. Riggs Flat is named for Col. Edwin A. Riggs who had his troops riding out of a temporary scouting camp in the region north of this mountain in the mid-1860s. To get to Riggs Flat, go south of Safford seven miles on U.S. Route 191, then turn right (west) onto State Route 366 (Swift Trail). Eventually the road becomes unpaved, very steep, and has numerous switchbacks. From Safford it's only 40-some miles to Riggs Flat, but the drive

(OPPOSITE) *Atop the 10,717-foot-tall Pinaleno Mountains, the trout in peaceful Riggs Flat Lake await the high-country angler.*
(ABOVE) *Top-of the-world views of southern Arizona's basin-and-range topography await at every turn on the Swift Trail up the northeast slope of the Pinalenos.*

probably will take 2 1/2 hours. There are no facilities of any kind. Make sure your gas tank is full.

⑫ **ROPER LAKE STATE PARK** has a surprise. Compared with some other places in Arizona, this general area is occasionally described by visitors as less than breathtaking. But if they spend the night here they will find the park has conveniences enough — ramadas, showers, and such — for local and international campers alike. Sycamore, cottonwood, tamarisk, and tules fringe the oasis-like 32-acre lake, while rainbow trout, largemouth bass, sunfish, and channel catfish swim in its waters. Ducks, coots, and other waterfowl paddle near the shore, and

the sky can suddenly fill with yellow-headed and red-winged blackbirds if a camper happens to startle them. At sunset the broad shoulders of the Pinaleno Mountains seem to swell against the western sky. And, oh yes, the surprise. Roper Lake State Park has a delightful, natural min-

eral springs hot tub. Get into your swimsuit and do a little relaxin'. To get here, drive six miles south of Safford on U.S. 191 and follow the sign.

⓭ **RUCKER CANYON** campgrounds spread out for about five miles along FR 74, 74E, and 74D in the southern reaches of the Chiricahua Mountains. The area is easily reached from Douglas by going north on U.S. Route 191 to about milepost 30 (Rucker Canyon Road). Turn east (right) for about 20 miles (the road will become FR 74) to Rucker Canyon. An alternate route is to go northeast from Douglas on State Route 80 about 30 miles to milepost 396. Then turn northwest (left) on Texas Canyon Road (which becomes FR 74) for about 15 miles. The roads in are unpaved but in good condition. Of the five campgrounds in the area, the following three are the author's favorites.

Camp Rucker, once called "Camp Supply," honors Lt. John A. Rucker. It is the first of the campgrounds encountered after turning onto FR 74E. During the 1880s Camp Rucker was one of a number of pivotal outposts that helped bring about the

surrender of Geronimo and his band of Apaches. From a purely practical point of view, it's easy to see why the Army picked this site: it's level, which makes it easy on horses and men, and a logical place to erect tents. Numerous trees shade the camp, including one cottonwood that looks old enough to have sheltered Rucker's troops.

(OPPOSITE, TOP) *Waters from natural hot springs bubble through the rock-lined hot tub at Roper Lake State Park campground.*
(OPPOSITE, BOTTOM) *The view from Roper Lake campground, near Safford, takes in the massive bulk of the Pinaleno Mountains and the Gila River Valley.*
(ABOVE) *At Camp Rucker you'll sleep among the memories of the Indian wars.*

⑭ **CYPRESS PARK** is next on FR 74E. It's another small, deeply shaded camp with a burbling brook, which makes it irresistible for me. Units are set among stately oaks and Arizona cypress trees. The latter, of course, inspired the campground's name. A sign at Cypress Park's entrance suggests that this place is popular with bears. Don't be careless. Put food and garbage in your car or closed containers before the campfire goes out. This is good advice to follow in all campgrounds in the Chiricahuas.

⑮ **RUCKER FOREST CAMP** lies at the head of Rucker Canyon at the end of FR 74D in the Chiricahua high country.

On the way in we saw a roadrunner, several hawks, some turkeys, hundrerds of small birds, numerous Chiricahua squirrels, and probably a dozen white-tailed deer. On 74D, you'll pass old Rucker Lake, which silted in after the Rattlesnake Fire in 1992. However, Rucker Creek still runs nearby, and there are several hiking trails near the camp.

⑯ **RUSTLER PARK**, at an elevation of 8,784 feet in the Chiricahua Mountains, is really a popular place. No matter when you go, expect company. In addition to campers, picnickers and sightseers make the trip. Why? Well, in late spring, for example, this mountain meadow may be "paved" with thousands of wild iris and the air filled with ladybugs. Despite

(OPPOSITE) *Nearby Camp Rucker's old cavalry stable still stands in the Chiricahua Mountains.* RANDY PRENTICE
(ABOVE) *One of the raptors that hunts the mountains and grasslands of southeastern Arizona from the wing, a hawk perches atop a fir tree.*

its remoteness, high elevation, and the twisting mountain roads you must travel to get here, I highly recommend it. If you had a time machine and could go back to the late 1870s and 80s, you would find that this prime mountain pasture was popular, as the name suggests, with rustlers. Rustler Park was a holding place for stolen cattle. Nefarious characters such as Johnny Ringo, Ike Clanton, the Frank McLowry Gang — all of O.K. Corral fame — conducted part of their "business" here. Today, it's unlikely you will see any rustlers, but cattle still graze in the area. To get here, follow the paved road west from Portal and in about five miles turn right onto unpaved FR 42. Nine miles farther, turn left (south) on FR 42D for three miles to Rustler Park.

⑰ SHANNON is up the Swift Trail 26 zigzag miles from Safford. At an elevation of about 9,000 feet, this is another pocket campground (10 units) in the pristine Pinaleno Mountains. A narrow gravel road leads into the campground where you're surrounded by firs, spruce, and aspens. To our surprise, the Forest Service had cut and left logs for firewood. You're guaranteed to see tassel-eared Abert squirrels, and there's a reasonable chance of spotting the threatened Mount Graham red squirrel.

STEWART (NO. 4), see Cave Creek Area, Page 169.
SUNNY FLAT (NO. 5), see Cave Creek Area.

18 SYCAMORE is a tiny five-unit campground at an elevation of about 6,200 feet in the Chiricahua Mountains. To get here, starting from the road to Chiricahua National Monument, take State Route 181 south about 10 miles. When S.R. 181 heads west, you go east onto unpaved FR 41. It leads across the treeless flats of Sulphur Springs Valley and zigzags upward, crossing Turkey Creek a couple of times. The creek flows most of the year, but under normal conditions it's no problem. Vegetation becomes dense and the forest closes in. About 10 miles after leaving the highway the shrubbery parts, and strad-

dling the stream is the grove of shapely trees responsible for the campground's signature. An important note for some of us: due to road conditions and the "closeness" of the forest, there is a 16-foot limit on trailers. Typical of sky-island campgrounds, there are many hiking trails in the vicinity. One of these leads to the Pole Bridge Canyon Nature Area.

(OPPOSITE) *Among the tall pines of the upper reaches of the Pinalenos, campers find Shannon campground cool and uncrowded.*
(ABOVE) *Sycamore campground on Turkey Creek in the lower elevations of the western Chiricahuas makes an excellent spring or autumn camp.*

REGION 8 FISHING	Dankworth Ponds	Eagle Creek (Lower)	Eagle Creek (Upper)	Riggs Flat Lake	Roper Lake	San Francisco River	San Carlos Lake
FACILITIES BOAT RENTAL					●		●
MOTOR LIMITS	elec				elec	elec	
BOATS ALLOWED	●			●	●	●	●
CAMP NEARBY			●	●	●	●	●
STORE							●
FISH SPECIES BULLHEAD							
CARP							
TILAPIA							
WALLEYE							
NORTHERN PIKE							
CATFISH (Flathead)						●	●
CATFISH (Channel)	●	●			●	●	●
SUNFISH	●				●		●
CRAPPIE					●		●
STRIPED BASS							
WHITE BASS							
SM.MOUTH BASS		●	●			●	
LG.MOUTH BASS	●				●		●
CUTTHROAT							
GRAYLING							
BROOK							
NATIVE							
BROWN				●			
RAINBOW			●	●	●		
FLY & LURE ONLY							
ELEVATION	3000	3000	5500	9000	3000	3500	2500
AVERAGE DEPTH (IN FEET)	15			45	20		
AVERAGE ACREAGE	10			11	32		18,000

(ABOVE) *Bass fishermen find 18,000-acre San Carlos Lake a hot spot northwest of Safford on the Gila River. The wide, shallow lake is on the San Carlos Apache Indian Reservation, and there is a small daily fee to fish or boat there.*

MANAGEMENT AGENCIES

Names and region numbers of campgrounds listed in italics

ASP

ARIZONA STATE PARKS
(602) 542-4174
1300 W. Washington St.
Phoenix, AZ 85007
www.azstateparks.com/parks/
 parklist.html

1. **Alamo Lake State Park**
   (928) 669-2088
   Alamo Lake, 4

2. **Buckskin Mountain State Park**
   (928) 667-3231
   Buckskin Mountain, 4

3. **Catalina State Park**
   (520) 628-5798
   Catalina, 7

4. **Cattail Cove State Park**
   (928) 855-1223
   Cattail Cove, 4

5. **Dead Horse Ranch State Park**
   (928) 634-5283
   Dead Horse Ranch, 2

6. **Homolovi Ruins State Park**
   (928) 289-4106
   Homolovi, 3

7. **Lost Dutchman State Park**
   (480) 982-4485
   Lost Dutchman, 5

8. **Lyman Lake State Park**
   (602) 337-4441
   Lyman Lake, 6

9. **Patagonia Lake State Park**
   (520) 287-6965
   Patagonia Lake, 7

10. **Picacho Peak State Park**
    (520) 466-3183
    Picacho Peak, 7

11. **Roper Lake State Park**
    (928) 428-6760
    Roper Lake, 8

12. **River Island Unit
    (Buckskin Mtn)**
    (928) 667-3386
    River Island, 4

BLM

BUREAU OF LAND MANAGEMENT
(602) 417-9300
222 N. Central Ave.
Phoenix, AZ 85004-2203
www.az.blm.gov/azmap.htm

1. **Arizona Strip Field Office**
   (435) 688-3200
   345 East Riverside Drive
   St. George, UT 84790-9000
   Virgin River, 1

2. **Kingman Field Office**
   (928) 718-3700
   2755 Mission Blvd.
   Kingman, AZ 86401
   Burro Creek, 4
   Wild Cow Springs, 4

3. **Phoenix Field Office**
   (623) 580-5500
   21605 N. 7th Av.
   Phoenix, AZ 85027-2099
   Painted Rock Petroglyph Site, 4

4. **Safford Field Office**
   (928) 348-4400
   711 14th Ave.
   Safford, AZ 85546-3321
   Fourmile Canyon, 8

CRP

COUNTY REGIONAL PARKS

1. **Maricopa County**
   (602) 506-2930
   411 N. Central Ave., Ste. 470
   Phoenix, AZ 85004
   www.maricopa.gov/parks

A. **McDowell Mountain Regional Park**
(480) 471-0173
McDowell Mountain Park, 5

B. **Usery Mountain Regional Park**
(480) 984-0032
Usery Mountain, 5

C. **White Tank Mountain Regional Park**
(623) 935-2505
White Tank, 5

2. **Mohave County**
(877) 757-0915
P.O. Box 7000
Kingman, AZ 86402
www.mcparks.com

A. **Davis Camp**
(928) 754-7250
Davis Camp, 4

B. **Hualapai Mountain Park**
(928) 757-3859
Hualapai Mountain Park, 4

3. **Pima County**
(520) 877-6000
3500 W. River Rd.
Tucson, AZ 85741
www.pima.gov/nrpr

A. **Tucson Mountain Park**
Gilbert Ray, 7

4. **Coconino County**
(928) 774-5139
HC 39 Box 3A
Flagstaff, AZ 86001
www.co.coconino.az.us/parks

A. **Fort Tuthill County Park**
(928) 774-3464
Fort Tuthill, 2

IJ
INDEPENDENT JURISDICTION

1. **Fishers Landing Campground**
(928) 539-9495
Fishers Landing, 4

IR
INDIAN RESERVATIONS

1. **White Mountain Apache Tribe Wildlife & Outdoor Recreation Division**
(928) 338-4385
P.O. Box 220
Whiteriver, AZ 85941
http://162.42.237.6/wmatod/index.htm
Drift Fence Lake, 6
Hawley Lake, 6
Lower Log Road, 6
Pacheta Lake, 6
Reservation Lake, 6
Shush Be Tou Lake, 6
Shush Be Zahze Lake, 6
Sunrise Lake, 6
Upper Log Road, 6

2. **Havasupai Tourist Enterprises**
(928) 448-2141
(928) 448-2121
P.O. Box 160
Supai, AZ 86435
www.havasupaitribe.com
Havasupai, 1

3. **Kaibab-Paiute Tribe**
(928) 643-7245
HC 65 Box 2
Fredonia, AZ 86022
www.kaibabpaiutetribal.com
Kaibab-Paiute Campground, 1

4. **Navajo Nation Parks & Recreation**
(928) 871-6647
Bldg. 36A E. Hwy. 264 @ Rte 12
Window Rock, AZ 86515
www.navajonationparks.org

A. **Monument Valley**
   Navajo Tribal Park
   (435) 727-5870
   Mitten View, 1

B. **Navajo Parks & Recreation**
   (928) 871-6636
   Wheatfields Lake, 1

5. **Hualapai Tribe**
   www.nps.gov/grca/crmp/documents/
   posters/Hualapai.pdf
   (928) 769-2227
   (928) 769-2219
   (888) 255-9550
   Peach Springs, AZ
   Diamond Creek, 1

NFS
NATIONAL FOREST SERVICE

1. **Apache-Sitgreaves**
   National Forests
   (928) 333-4301
   P.O. Box 640
   Springerville, AZ 85938
   www.fs.fed.us/r3/asnf

   A. **Alpine Ranger District**
      (928) 339-4384
      Alpine Divide, 6
      Benny Creek, 6
      Diamond Rock, 6
      Hannagan, 6
      Luna Lake, 6

   B. **Black Mesa Ranger District**
      (928) 535-4481
      Aspen, 3
      Spillway, 3
      Bear Canyon Lake, 3
      Black Canyon Rim, 3
      Canyon Point, 3
      FR 9350, 3

   C. **Clifton Ranger District**
      (928) 687-1301
      Honeymoon, 6
      Horseshoe Cienega, 6
      K.P. Cienega, 6
      Upper Blue, 6

D. **Springerville Ranger District**
   (928) 333-4372
   Big Lake Recreation Area, 6
   Blue Crossing, 6
   Buffalo Crossing, 6
   Rolfe C. Hoyer, 6
   South Fork, 6
   West Fork, 6
   Winn, 6

E. **Lakeside Ranger District**
   (928) 368-5111
   Los Burros, 6

2. **Coconino National Forest**
   (928) 527-3600
   1824 S. Thompson St.
   Flagstaff, AZ 86001
   www.fs.fed.us/r3/coconino

   A. **Mogollon Rim**
      Ranger District
      (928) 477-2172
      (928) 477-2255
      Blue Ridge, 3
      Clints Well, 3
      Kehl Springs, 3
      Knoll Lake, 3
      Long Lake, 3
      Rock Crossing, 3

   B. **Mormon Lake**
      Ranger District
      (928) 774-1147
      Dairy Spring, 2
      Double Springs, 2
      Forked Pine, 2
      Kinnikinick Lake, 2
      Lake View, 2
      Pine Grove, 2

   C. **Peaks Ranger District**
      (928) 526-0866
      Bonito, 2

   D. **Red Rock Ranger District**
      (928) 282-4119
      Beaver Creek, 2
      Cave Springs, 2
      Pine Flat, 2

3. Coronado National Forest
(520) 388-8300
300 West Congress St.
Tucson, AZ 85701
www.fs.fed.us/r3/coronado

A. Douglas Ranger District
(520) 364-3468
Idlewilde, 8
Stewart, 8
Sunny Flat, 8
Cochise Stronghold, 8
Herb Martyr, 8
Pinery Canyon, 8
Camp Rucker, 8
Cypress Park, 8
Rucker Forest Camp, 8
Rustler Park, 8
Sycamore, 8

B. Nogales Ranger District
(520) 281-2296
Bog Springs, 7

C. Safford Ranger District
(928) 428-4150
Arcadia, 8
Hospital Flat, 8
Riggs Flat, 8
Shannon, 8

D. Santa Catalina Ranger District
(520) 749-8700
Molino Basin, 7
Peppersauce, 7
Rose Canyon, 7
Spencer Canyon, 7

E. Sierra Vista Ranger District
(520) 378-0311
Lakeview, 7
Ramsey Vista, 7
Reef Townsite, 7

4. Kaibab National Forest
(928) 635-8200
800 S. 6th St.
Williams, AZ 86046
www.fs.fed.us/r3/kai

A. North Kaibab Ranger District
(928) 643-7395
Demotte, 1
Jacob Lake, 1
Indian Hollow, 1

B. Tusayan Ranger District
(928) 638-2443
Ten-X, 1

C. Williams Ranger District
(928) 635-5600
Dogtown Lake, 2
Kaibab Lake, 2
White Horse Lake, 2

5. Prescott National Forest
(928) 443-8000
344 S. Cortez St.
Prescott, AZ 86303
www.fs.fed.us/r3/prescott

A. Bradshaw Ranger District
(928) 443-8000
Hazlett Hollow, 2
Hilltop, 2
Lower Wolf Creek, 2
Lynx Lake, 2
White Spar, 2
Yavapai, 2

B. Verde Ranger District
(928) 567-4121
Mingus Mountain, 2
Potato Patch, 2
Powell Springs, 2

6. Tonto National Forest
(602) 225-5200
2324 E. McDowell Road
Phoenix, AZ 85006
www.fs.fed.us/r3/tonto

A. Cave Creek Ranger District
(480) 595-3300
Seven Springs, 5

B. Globe Ranger District
(928) 402-6200
Pinal, 5

C. Mesa Ranger District
(480) 610-3300
Tortilla, 5

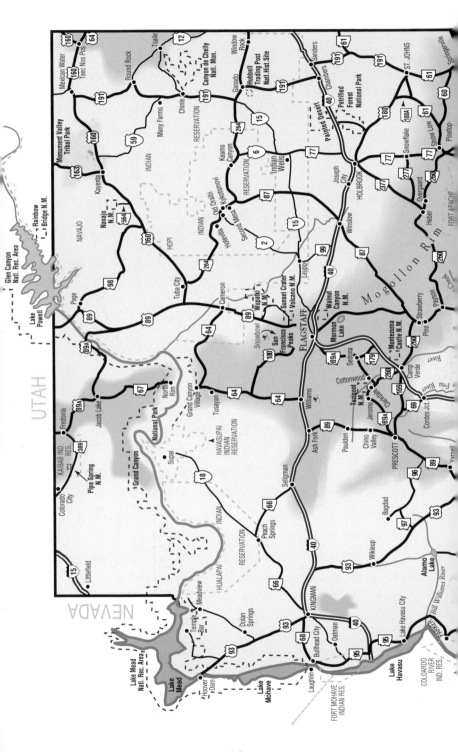

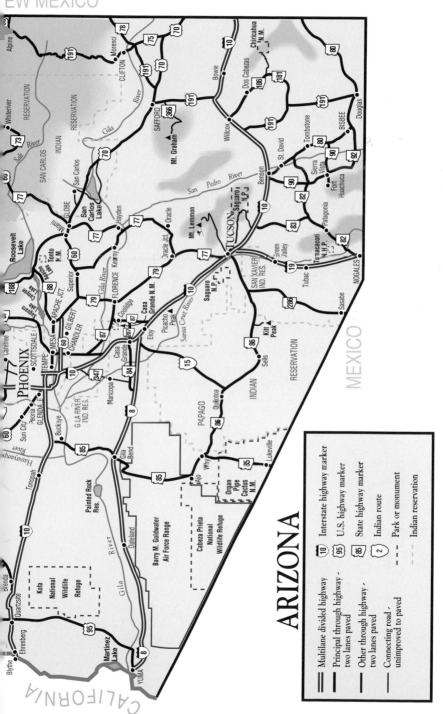

ARIZONA

- ═══ Multilane divided highway
- ─── Principal through highway - two lanes paved
- ─── Other through highway - two lanes paved
- ─── Connecting road - unimproved to paved
- 🛡10 Interstate highway marker
- 🛡95 U.S. highway marker
- 🛡85 State highway marker
- 🛡2 Indian route
- --- Park or monument
- --- Indian route
- --- Indian reservation

MANAGEMENT AGENCIES

D. **Payson Ranger District**
(928) 474-7900
Christopher Creek, 3
Ponderosa, 3

E. **Pleasant Valley**
Ranger District
(928) 462-4300
Airplane Flat, 3
Valentine Ridge, 3
Rose Creek, 5

F. **Tonto Basin Ranger District**
(928) 467-3200
Burnt Corral, 5
Cholla Recreation Site, 5
Schoolhouse Point, 5
Windy Hill, 5

NATIONAL PARK SERVICE
www.nps.gov/parks.html

1. **Canyon de Chelly**
National Monument
(928) 674-5500
www.nps.gov/cach/
Cottonwood, 1

2. **Chiricahua**
National Monument
(520) 824-3560
www.nps.gov/chir/
Bonita Canyon, 8

3. **Glen Canyon National**
Recreation Area
(928) 355-2234
(928) 645-1059
www.nps.gov/glca/
Lee's Ferry, 1
Wahweap, 1

4. **Grand Canyon National Park**
www.nps.gov/grca/

A. **Backcountry Camping**
www.nps.gov/grca/backcountry
(928) 638-7875
Bright Angel, 1
Cottonwood Camp, 1
Indian Garden, 1

B. **Rim Camping**
www.nps.gov/grca/grandcanyon
(800) 365-2267
Desert View, 1
Mather, 1
North Rim, 1
Toroweap Point, 1

5. **Lake Mead**
National Recreation Area
www.nps.gov/lame

A. **Katherine Landing**
Ranger Station
(928) 754-3272
Katherine Landing, 4

B. **Temple Bar**
(928) 767-3211
Temple Bar, 4

6. **Navajo National Monument**
(928) 672-2700
www.nps.gov/nava/
Navajo National Monument, 1

7. **Organ Pipe Cactus**
National Monument
(520) 387-6849
www.nps.gov/orpi/
Organ Pipe Cactus National
Monument, 4

National Recreation
Reservation Services
Toll free telephone: (877) 444-6777
(800) 365-2267
TDD: (877) 833-6777
International: (518) 885-3639
(301) 722-1257
Online: www.ReserveUSA.com
http://reservations.nps.gov